CURRICULUM DESIGN FOR THE SEVERELY AND PROFOUNDLY HANDICAPPED

CURRICULUM DESIGN FOR THE SEVERELY AND PROFOUNDLY HANDICAPPED

Paul Wehman, Ph.D.

Virginia Commonwealth University

HUMAN SCIENCES PRESS
72 Fifth Avenue   3 Henrietta Street
NEW YORK, NY 10011 ● LONDON, WC2E 8LU

Library of Congress Catalog Number 78-23704

ISBN: 0-87705-365-0

Copyright © 1979 by Human Sciences Press
72 Fifth Avenue, New York, New York 10011

Printed in the United States of America

9 987654321

Library of Congress Cataloging in Publication Data

Wehman, Paul.
    Curriculum design for the severely and profoundly handicapped.

    Bibliography: p.
    Includes index.
    1. Mentally handicapped children—Education—United States. 2. Curriculum planning—United States. I. Title.
LC4601.W395   371.9'284   78-23704
ISBN 0-87705-365-0

To
Jo Ann Marchant and Geraldine Brandon for their help
and support

CONTENTS

7

LIST OF FIGURES

13

LIST OF TABLES

ACKNOWLEDGMENTS

I have written *Curriculum Design for the Severely and Profoundly Handicapped* primarily to synthesize the current literature in the area of education and training programs for the severely and profoundly handicapped. I would like to thank several students for their task analysis and instructional program contributions. Cheryl Broga, Melinda Ferk, Jeannie Donovan, Linda Abbey, Betty Neale, Nancy Sanders, Phyllis Brocklehurst, and Jo Anne Taylor are among some of the students who developed instructional programs under my supervision.

I also drew heavily on the technical assistance of Carol Granger and Sharon Garrett in the motor development and language skill areas. These professionals are now contributing to the excellent program for the severely and profoundly handicapped which is developing at Hickory Hill School in Richmond, Virginia, under the supervision of Mrs. Geraldine Brandon.

I am most indebted to Jo Ann Marchant for her practical suggestions and guidelines for instruction, particularly in Chapter 2 on self-help skills. She has proven to be an exemplary model of teaching for me.

Finally, I want to thank Charlotte Parks who typed the manuscript and, as usual, was extremely quick, efficient, and pleasant throughout the whole process.

Chapter 1

INTRODUCTION

Educational programming for the severely and profoundly handicapped is currently the most pressing area in special education. The Bureau of Education for the Handicapped (BEH) has identified education and treatment of the severely handicapped as a top priority in response to the Education for All Handicapped Children Act, which was enacted in 1975. In light of this federal mandate, state and local education agencies have begun to deliver instructional services to handicapped children who have previously been excluded from the public schools.

Those children who typically have been rejected by public school systems are usually not toilet-trained, display severe behavior problems, are nonverbal, are grossly delayed in self-help, social, and motor skill development, and may suffer from severe physical or sensory impairments (Sontag, Burke, & York, 1973). Frequently, measured intelligence (IQ) is below 35. BEH estimates that there are presently 1.5 million severely and profoundly handicapped individuals in the country. The educational needs of these persons can be met only by teacher training programs specially designed for dealing with them. Retraining of previously certified special education teachers who were trained to work with the mildly handicapped will also be necessary (Brown & York, 1974; Stainback, Stainback, & Maurer, 1976).

THE NEED FOR TEACHER TRAINING

There are at least three major reasons why massive training of teachers is necessary for the education of severely and profoundly handicapped individuals. First, the curriculum content of relevant educational programs is, in short, radically different from classroom programs for nonhandicapped and mildly handicapped students. Instead of learning reading, writing, and arithmetic, severely involved children must first learn how to walk, communicate, eat, use the toilet, dress, and interact socially. These skills are major landmarks for many severely handicapped children and thus make up the educational curriculum. The chapters in this book reflect the principal curriculum areas required in most comprehensive educational programs for severely involved students.

A second reason for the specialized training of personnel is that more powerful instructional procedures are needed to effect a positive behavior change in students. Usually, severely handicapped students do not learn as rapidly as mildly handicapped or nonhandicapped students. The more precise teaching procedures required must involve the psychology of learning, and specifically operant and discrimination learning. There is increasing evidence to support the efficacy of those learning principles with severely handicapped students. Principles of task analysis, behavior shaping, prompting, fading, modeling, imitation training, discrimination, and generalization are clearly an effective means of intervention. Unfortunately, many teacher training programs do not emphasize these competencies; therefore new teachers as well as those already in the field do not exhibit these powerful types of intervention procedures. Although this book is not specifically a behavior modification text, instructional guidelines and sample programs are included in each chapter to help the teacher become familiar with available resources.

A third major reason for retraining is that it will be necessary for teachers to follow up classroom programs into the home with families. The severely handicapped child has traditionally been institutionalized, and if school programs such as toilet training or behavior control are not pursued in the home, the child will behave appropriately only when in school. Parents cannot be expected to have the necessary skills to deal with their severely involved child. They must be aware of (1) their rights and due process; (2) what makes up a *relevant* educational curriculum for their child; (3) what they should realistically expect from their child; (4) how they can help facilitate instructional programs begun at school; and (5) how they can control their child at home and in the community.

Only trained professionals can help the parents adjust to living with the severely involved child. The best way to promote this adjustment process is not only through counseling, but through teaching the parent how to manage the child.

WHY EDUCATION FOR THE SEVERELY HANDICAPPED CHILD?

There are already a significant number of administrators and teachers in regular and special education who do not feel that education for severely and profoundly handicapped children justifies a large expenditure of money when financial resources are extremely limited. Many of these people can and do have a substantial influence on the direction of public policy. So as a prelude to this text on curriculum, it is important to explain why severely involved children must receive a public school education along with their nonhandicapped and mildly handicapped peers.

For the longest time, severely and profoundly handicapped persons have been shunned, neglected, rejected, and excluded from education and rehabilitation services. The purported reason for this neglect is that they cannot learn or will never make contributions to society. This allegation is not true. Far too much literature in recent years indicates quite the opposite. The severely and profoundly handicapped can learn vocational skills (Bellamy, 1976; Brown, Certo, Belmore, & Crowner, 1976; Gold, 1976; Karan, Wehman, Renzaglia, & Schutz, 1976), leisure skills (Wehman, 1977), motor skills (Brown, Scheuerman, & Crowner, 1976), preacademic skills (Brown, Crowner, Williams, & York, 1975), language (Bricker, Ruder, & Vincent, 1976), and self-care skills (Gardner, 1971). The question is not whether they can learn or will they make a contribution, but *how much* can they learn and how quickly, and how ready society is to accept them.

The fact is that no one knows the answer to these questions. Public school education for the severely and profoundly handicapped has been in full force for very few years, and in some states it still has not begun. It will take a full generation of students (18 years) and an accumulation of longitudinal data before we can state just what potential the more severely involved student has. Until that time, at least, it is imperative that these students be given every chance to develop.

Purpose of Text

As might be expected, an increasing volume of literature has been directed to the needs of teachers and other practitioners who work directly with the severely and profoundly handicapped. Because of the complex learning and behavior problems which many of these individuals display, there is a critical need for information relating to instructional techniques. A careful review of the textbook literature in this area, however, reveals that many of the books either take the "cookbook" approach, in which instructional programs or curricula are listed with little explanation of or rationale for these skills (Adams, 1974; Anderson, Hodson, & Jones, 1974; Baldwin, et al., 1976; Myers, Sinco, & Stalma, 1973), or are edited books with collections of reprinted journal articles (e.g., Gibson & Brown, 1976). These books represent a necessary beginning to the dissemination of the information available for training children with severe behavioral handicaps. Unfortunately, they do not review the relevant literature which provides the knowledge base for instructional technology with severely handicapped students. And they do not merge the research findings into adaptable instructional guidelines and curriculum design.

It is the intent of this text to identify and describe relevant curriculum areas, such as self-help, motor, social, language, and vocational skills. This book is designed for special education teachers, psychologists, occupational therapists, administrators, and other professionals involved in educating severely and profoundly handicapped students. Although it is not the expressed purpose of this book to describe behavior modification techniques, several chapters include sample programs and detailed instructional guidelines for implementing relevant training programs.

References

Adams, J. *An education curriculum for the moderately, severely and profoundly mentally handicapped pupil.* Springfield, Illinois: Charles C. Thomas, 1974.

Anderson, D., Hodson, G., & Jones, W. *Instructional programming for the handicapped student.* Springfield, Illinois: Charles C. Thomas, 1974.

Baldwin, V., et al. *The teaching research curriculum for moderately and severely handicapped.* Springfield, Illinois: Charles C. Thomas, 1976.

Bellamy, G. T. (Ed.) *Habilitation of severely and profoundly retarded adults.* Eugene, Oregon: Center on Human Development, University of Oregon, 1976.

Bricker, D. D., Ruder, K., & Vincent, B. An intervention strategy for language-deficient children. In N. Haring & R. Schiefelbusch (Eds.), *Teaching Special Children,* New York: McGraw-Hill, 1976.

Brown, L., Crowner, T., Williams, W., & York, R. *Madison's alternative to zero exclusion: A book of readings.* Madison, Wisconsin: Madison Public Schools, 1975.

Brown, L., Scheuerman, N., & Crowner, T. *Madison's alternative to zero exclusion: Toward an integrated therapy model for teaching motor, tracking, and scanning skills to severely handicapped students.* Madison, Wisconsin: Madison Public Schools, 1976.

Brown, L., & York, R. Developing programs for severely handicapped students: Teacher training and classroom instruction. *Focus on Exceptional Children,* 1974, *6(2).*

Brown, L., Certo, N., Belmore, K., & Crowner, T. *Madison's alternative to zero exclusion: Papers and programs related to public school services for secondary age severely handicapped students.* Madison, Wisconsin: Madison Public Schools, 1976.

Gardner, W. I. *Behavior modification in mental retardation.* Chicago, Illinois: Aldine-Atherton, 1971.

Gibson, D., & Brown, R. (Eds.) *Managing the severely retarded.* Springfield, Illinois: Charles C. Thomas, 1976.

Gold, M. W. Task analysis of a complex assembly task by the retarded blind. *Exceptional Children,* 1976, *43(2),* 78–85.

Karan, O. C., Wehman, P., Renzaglia, A., & Schutz, R. *Habilitation practices with the severely developmentally disabled.* Madison, Wisconsin: University of Wisconsin Rehabilitation Research and Training Center, 1976.

Myers, D., Sinco, R., & Stalma, M. *The right-to-education child.* Springfield, Illinois: Charles C. Thomas, 1973.

Sontag, E., Burke, P., & York, R. Consideration for serving the severely handicapped in the public school. *Education and Training of the Mentally Retarded,* 1973, *8*, 20–26.

Stainback, S., Stainback, W., & Maurer, S. Training teachers for the severely and profoundly handicapped: A new frontier. *Exceptional Children,* 1976, *42(4),* 203–210.

Wehman, P. *Helping the mentally retarded acquire play skills: A behavioral approach.* Springfield, Illinois: Charles C. Thomas, 1977.

Chapter 2

SELF-HELP SKILLS

Teaching self-care skills to the severely and profoundly handicapped is an important step in dispelling the notion that individuals with severe behavioral handicaps cannot learn. Furthermore, the development and maintenance of self-help skills promotes deinstitutionalization and lends credibility to the recent right-to-education mandate provided for all handicapped children (Gilhool, 1976).

In the previous decade, a series of clinical reports and a limited number of controlled research studies have investigated the acquisition and performance of toileting, eating, dressing, and grooming skills in severely and profoundly handicapped persons (e.g., Gardner, 1971). However, few reports review the progress made in each of these areas, and more importantly, few describe the interaction of variables such as chronological age, sex, and institutionalization of subjects, training procedures, response measures, and length of training times. To bridge the gap between research and clinical/instructional activity by practitioners, a descriptive analysis and synthesis of the self-help skill training studies is presented. This chapter briefly reviews relevant research in the major self-care skills. It evaluates the studies performed and provides specific instructional guidelines to follow in teaching each skill.

TOILET TRAINING

Many toilet-training programs have been documented since the early operant work by Ellis (1963) and Dayan (1964). There are also several reviews that discuss the merits and weaknesses of the toilet-training studies conducted in the past decade (Osarchuk, 1973; Rentfrow & Rentfrow, 1969).

The basic operant strategy employed in training toileting skills is behavior shaping or the method of successive approximations. The efficiency of this method has been supported by numerous investigators (Baumeister & Klosowski, 1975; Gelbert & Meyer, 1965; Giles & Wolf, 1966; Hundziak, Maurer, & Watson, 1965; Kimbrell, Luckey, Barbuto, & Love, 1967; Levine & Elliot, 1970; Mahoney, Van Wagenen, & Meyerson, 1971).

Essentially what is involved is the sequencing of the skills required for toileting: finding the toilet, pulling down the pants, sitting on the toilet, defecating or urinating, using tissue paper, pulling up the pants, flushing the toilet, and washing and drying the hands. Training usually includes contingent reinforcement of each of these steps by a supervisor. Careful data and records are kept to indicate progress being made.

Although applications of operant conditioning to toilet training have been successful, recent advances in behavior modification have led to even more dramatic improvement in the speed and effectiveness with which toileting skills can be acquired (Foxx & Azrin, 1973). As

Azrin and Foxx (1971) note, many of the previous studies performed in the 1960s failed to provide conclusive follow-up data, and thus the maintenance of newly acquired toileting skills was suspect.

The Azrin and Foxx rapid method of toilet training decreased training times to approximately 4 to 5 days. There are six distinctive features of this approach:

1. The frequency of urination is artificially increased by providing more liquids.
2. Positive reinforcement is given for appropriate toilet use; however, toileting accidents result in a brief time-out.
3. An apparatus fastened to the pants and toilet automatically signals moisture or elimination of the stool.
4. "Full cleanliness training" requires that the child clean up thoroughly after an accident.
5. Self-initiated toileting is encouraged.
6. Positive reinforcement is given for being dry.

The emphasis on self-initiated or independent toileting is an important milestone in toilet training of the severely and profoundly handicapped. This aspect of training eliminates the need for external prompts or control, and develops independent behavior in the individual. The Azrin and Foxx (1971) report also includes a fully described maintenance procedure.

Toilet training studies that have been conducted with the severely and profoundly retarded are listed in Table 2-1. Several parameters of these investigations were identified: number of individuals participating in study, sex and age of individuals, history of institutionalization, type of research design, principal independent and dependent variables utilized, and length of time for completion of study. (This analysis is discussed and other self-care areas

Table 2–1. Toilet Training Studies

Study	Sample size	Subject characteristics	Institutionalization	Research design	Teaching procedures	Response measure	Length of study or training time
Dayan (1964)	25	Severe/profound retardation; 6–12 years old	Yes	Clinical study; no control group	Food reinforcement plus attention for appropriate voiding; ignoring soiling	Pounds of soiled linen per resident	1 year
Baumeister & Klosowski (1965)	11	Severe/profound retardation; 10–25 years old	Yes	Clinical study; no control group	Food reinforcement for appropriate responses in toileting chain, with emphasis on correct voiding in commode	Frequency of urination and defecation	70 days
Gelbert & Myer (1965)	1	No retardation; 13-year-old boy	No	Clinical study; no control group	Activity reinforcement for appropriate defecation	Soiled pants checked four times daily	52 days

Study	N	Population		Design	Treatment	Measure	Duration
Hundziak, Maurer, & Watson (1968)	29	7–14-year-old boys	Yes	Experimental/control (operant vs. conventional training)	Automatically delivered positive reinforcement for appropriate urination or defecation	Frequency of accidents	5½ days
Giles & Wolf (1966)	5	Severe retardation; boys	Yes	AB	Positive reinforcement and physical restraint	Frequency soiled, frequency of other-initiated and self-initiated toiletings	56 days
Kimbrell, Luckey, Barbuto, & Love (1967)	40	Severe/profound retardation; 5–18-year-old girls	Yes	Experimental/control group	Food reinforcement for appropriate voiding	Gains made on Vineland social maturity scale; amount of laundry used	7 months
Levine & Elliot (1970)	103	Profound retardation; males/females, 4–48 years old	Yes	Clinical study; no control group	Positive reinforcement for voiding in commode	Number of accidental defecations	10 weeks
Azrin & Foxx (1971)	9	Profound retardation; sex not described	Yes	AB	Positive reinforcement plus positive practice and full cleanliness training	Frequency of toileting accidents per day	56 days with 90 day follow up (effective within 7 days)

30

Study	N	Subjects	Clinical study	Design	Treatment	Measure	Results
Mahoney, Van Wagenen & Meyerson (1971)	8	3 nonretarded infants and 5 severely retarded children	No		Positive reinforcement of each component in toileting chain	Number of steps in toileting task analysis acquired	Recorded hours and trials; days not available
Azrin, Sneed, & Foxx (1973)	12	Severe retardation; adults	Yes	Comparison between urine-alarm vs. dry bed techniques	Positive reinforcement plus positive practice and full cleanliness training	Percentage of nights bed was wet	84 days (effective within 7 days)
Foxx & Azrin (1973)	34	Nonhandicapped children with a mean age of 25 months	No	AB	Positive reinforcement plus modeling with positive practice and full cleanliness training		7 days with 4-month follow-up (effective in 2 days)

			Experimental/ control				
Azrin, Sneed, & Foxx (1974)	24	Nonhandicapped children with a mean age of 8 years	No		Positive reinforcement plus positive practice and full cleanliness training	Median bedwettings per week	28 days plus 4-month follow-up
Doleys & Arnold (1975)	1	Profound retardation; 8-year-old boy	No	AB	Positive reinforcement plus full cleanliness training	Frequency of soiling and bowel movements per week	98 days
Smith, Britton, Johnson, & Thomas (1975)	5	Profound retardation; adults	Yes	AB	Positive reinforcement plus positive practice and full cleanliness training	Frequency of self-initiations to toilet and frequency of wetting accidents	63 days

are evaluated later in this chapter.) It should be noted that in many cases several independent variables were in evidence. An effort was made to identify the most distinctive feature of the change procedures employed and to report this as the independent variable.

Eating Skills

Development of appropriate eating behavior is a programming area that has received increased attention in recent years. Several reports describe the acquisition of independent spoon feeding by dividing the behavior into smaller steps (Berkowitz, Sherry, & Davis, 1971; Christian, Holloman, & Lanier, 1973; Groves & Carroccio, 1971; Henrikson & Doughty, 1967; Zeiler & Jervey, 1968). With a backward chaining of responses, students are initially physically guided through most of the spoon feeding and are required only to empty the spoon into their mouth. As the child becomes more proficient, the trainer gradually fades hand support until total independence is achieved.

A critical component in most of these programs is a time-out period or temporary removal of the food as punishment for inappropriate eating. The experimental efficacy of this procedure has been demonstrated with a series of socially unacceptable eating behaviors such as "pigging" and food stealing (Barton, Guess, Garcia, & Baer, 1970).

Physical restraints have also been used temporarily with children who constantly grab food with their free hand (Song & Gandhi, 1974). Song and Gandhi have suggested that the developmental levels of arm and hand movement are important factors in deciding which children are good candidates for training.

The work of Azrin and his associates provides direction for the training and maintenance of eating skills in the profoundly retarded (O'Brien & Azrin, 1972; O'Brien, Bugle & Azrin, 1972). This research also emphasizes the critical role of maintenance procedures.

A major distinction between the research programs of Azrin's group and those of other workers is that eating training includes a full chain of eating skills. Students are trained in the use of napkins, utensils, and other meal-time accessories. One example of the success of this method is the "mini-meal" approach to the rapid training of eating to the profoundly retarded (Azrin & Armstrong, 1973). The "mini-meal" approach divides the three daily meals into a number of shorter meals throughout the day. In this way the child receives numerous opportunities for training and practicing appropriate eating behavior. Furthermore, the problem of satiation encountered in using three large meals for training is minimized.

Table 2–2 is an analysis of the available eating studies. The parameters examined were similar to those in the toilet-training analysis. However, since socially unacceptable eating behavior is a common problem with the severely retarded, studies that describe procedures to ameliorate inappropriate eating or refusal to eat are also identified.

INSTRUCTIONAL GUIDELINES FOR EATING

When to Feed the Child

1. At the beginning of feeding training, take the child by himself or herself. Be sure to give undivided attention and as much time as necessary.
2. As children advance, graduate them to eating before the family meal, and then let them sit with the family, eating a cracker, for example.
3. Feeding training always should be a pleasant experience. It should be done when the child is

Table 2-2. Studies of Eating Training

Study	Sample size	Subject characteristics	Institutionalization	Research design	Teaching procedures	Response measure	Length of study or training time
Henrikson & Doughty (1967)	4	Profoundly retarded boys	Yes	Clinical study; no control group	Verbal disapproval, facial disapproval, physical interruption	Frequency of weekly eating misbehaviors	13 weeks
Zeiler & Jervey (1968)	1	Profoundly retarded 15-year-old girl	Yes	Clinical study; no control group	Backward chaining with food on spoon as reinforcer	Percentage of self-fed spoonfuls	46 sessions
Stolz & Wolf (1969)	1	Severely retarded 16-year-old blind boy	Yes	AB with brief reversal periods	Positive reinforcement, i.e., visual discrimination training	Percentage of correct responses of component skills involved in eating in a cafeteria	50 sessions
Barton, Guess, Garcia, & Baer (1970)	16	Severe/profound retardation; adolescent males	Yes	Multiple baseline across behaviors	Praise plus 15-second tray removal and also time-out from whole meal	Frequency of food stealing, fingers in food, and "pigging"	120 meals

Study	N	Population		Design	Treatment	Dependent measure	Duration
Groves & Carroccio (1971)	60	Severe/profound retardation; men and women	Yes	Changing criterion	Positive reinforcement plus 10-second tray removal	Number of hand-to-food responses allowed; mean number of residents removed per meal per day	98 days
Berkowitz, Sherry, & Davis (1971)	14	Profound retardation; 9–17-year-olds	Yes	Clinical study; no control	Backward chaining with food on spoon as reinforcer	Independent spoon feeding	2–60 days
Martin, McDonald, & Ominchinski (1971)	4	Severe retardation; 9–19-year-old girls	Yes	Baseline; time-out, reversal 1; time-out, reversal 2; time-out	Food removal (i.e., time-out) for inappropriate eating	Frequency of yelling, slopping, hands in food, and playing with utensils	100 sessions
O'Brien, Bugle, & Azrin (1972)	1	Profound retardation; 6-year-old girl	Yes	ABAB	Praise plus tray removal plus 5 daily meals instead of 3	Percentage of correct feeding responses	70 sessions
O'Brien & Azrin (1972)	11	Severe retardation; adults	Yes	Experimental/control group	Manual guidance plus instruction, or imitation plus instruction, or instruction only	Eating errors as percentage of total eating responses	Acquisition occurred in mean of 7 meals; 4 weeks of maintenance training

Table 2–2. (Continued)

Study	Sample size	Subject characteristics	Institutionalization	Research design	Teaching procedures	Response measure	Length of study or training time
Christian, Holloman, & Lanier (1973)	28	Severe/profound retardation; women	Yes	AB	Praise plus 10-second tray removal for inappropriate eating	Frequency of hand-to-food response; eating directly from tray; food stealing	45 days
Azrin & Armstrong (1973)	22	Profound retardation; adult men, mean age 38	Yes	AB with an experimental/control comparison between "minimeal" and conventional eating training	Praise plus increased meals plus positive practice plus completeness of training (i.e., cutting, buttering, etc.)	Number of residents trained; frequency of eating errors	18 days (9 meals per day)
Song & Gandhi (1974)	4	Severe retardation; children	Yes	AB	Praise plus 1-minute tray removal	Percentage of correct independent spoon-feeding cycles	15 weeks

Madsen, Madsen, & Thompson (1974)	46	Rural black children, culturally disadvantaged	No	ABAB	Praise plus candy	Average percentage of food consumed	18 days
Eaton & Brown (1974)	4	Mild to moderate retardation; adults	Yes	Pre-posttest	Modeling plus social and penny reinforcement	Keeping feet on floor; slouching on chair; eating too fast; eating with mouth open	Not reported
Nelson, Cone, & Hanson (1975)	24	Severe retardation; mean age—13 years	Yes	ABCD	Modeling vs. physical guidance	Percentage of time correct utensil was used	50 days
Jackson, Johnson, Ackron, & Crowley (1975)	2	Profound retardation; adult males	Yes	ABAB	Satiation	Frequency of vomiting	48 sessions

ready, and, to a certain extent, it should respect the child's preference for different foods. Introduce new food slowly and always let it be accompanied by a familiar one.

Positioning

Feeding in the correct position should start as soon as possible. When teaching parents of very young children, it is important to give clear and detailed instructions to *both* parents, if at all possible.

1. The child's head should be in a slightly downward position (the normal position during eating).
2. The spoon (with a small shallow bowl in the beginning) should be placed into the mouth from either side rather than directly from the front, with a slight downward pressure to counteract the common tongue thrust.
3. Encourage the child to take the food from the spoon with the lips and not with the teeth.
4. To assist swallowing, stroke the child's throat slightly. If the child gags or chokes, put the head forward and down. The child will probably throw the head back and put a stretch on the esophagus, preventing the food from getting dislodged.
5. The child should sit in a correct position, with the feet supported and the elbows resting on the table. It may be necessary to use special supports such as straps and sandbags to secure proper position. However, keep such measures to a minimum, because it may be hard to wean the child away from them later.

Swallowing

To teach voluntary swallowing, the following steps should be followed:

1. The head should be in slightly downward position.
2. Use only a small amount of liquid in the cup; it is easier and keeps the child from being discouraged.
3. Stroke the throat to facilitate swallowing.
4. Discourage the child from biting the cup.
5. If there is no lip closure (due to overbite or involuntary motion), hold the lips shut with very slight finger pressure to the upper and lower lips.
6. Teach the child to take one sip and swallow.
7. If the child stiffens as the cup approaches, wait until he relaxes again. He will soon learn that he will get food only when relaxed.

Straw-Drinking

Straw-drinking can be started whether the hands are ready or not. There are several important factors to remember:

1. It is a step towards independent feeding.
2. It is a prespeech activity (breath control for example).
3. It helps in controlling drooling.
4. It is an excellent means of getting liquids into a severely involved child.

    A. Use a short plastic straw with a small circumference.
    B. Only a small amount of liquid should be placed in the cup.

C. Let the child take only one sip at the time, gradually increasing speed until it becomes a continuous procedure.

D. Encourage the child to close only his lips and not his teeth. If lip closure is not present or is insufficient, again apply slight pressure with your fingers to the lips around the straw.

E. A good way to start is to use a small Tupperware cup, with a lid that has a straw running through it. It is possible to push milk into the child's mouth by pressing on the lid, after which the child will swallow and gradually get the idea of sucking up. Karo syrup applied to the tip of the straw also encourages sucking. Later, several small holes may be punched in the lid to allow easier flow.

F. Increase the length of the straw and change to liquid with a heavier flow, like milkshakes, as the child progresses.

G. Use a paper straw and see how many the child needs to empty a cup.

Using a Cup

Use a lipped-plastic or tin cup with a big handle, and put only a small amount of liquid into it. At first assist the child in holding the cup; later let the child try by himself, even if he spills.

Chewing

Start with semisolid foods (lima beans, carrots, etc.) that the child likes. Bread or vanilla crackers are soft and prevent choking. With each bite, encourage the child to chew before swallowing until it becomes a habit. By putting food between the teeth from alternate sides of the mouth, you hope to set off the chewing reflex by stimulating the inside of the cheek. The same method seems to counteract tongue thrust. Give more and more solid foods as chewing strength increases.

Self-Feeding

1. Assistive devices can be utilized to facilitate self-feeding:

   A. A built-up handle on a spoon is helpful, as is a handcuff to hold the spoon. Use the fork as much as possible, since it is easier to spear food than to get it onto a spoon.
   B. A plate with sides will make food fall back onto the plate.
   C. A cut-out board can be used to hold the plate if necessary.
   D. Use a cup that is not too large and has a lip.
   E. A cup-holder is called for if the child cannot hold cup.
   F. Try something sticky at first, like mashed potatoes, or something that will not fall off the spoon so easily.

2. Several points are important to remember in feeding training:

   A. Be sure of good body position.
   B. If indicated, stabilize the feet and the other hand.
   C. Support hands on the table.
   D. Let the child figure out which hands he wants to use.
   E. Make a dry run until the child is familiar with the activity and understands exactly what is expected.

F.   Give the child some assistance at first, then gradually reduce it.

G.   Let the child try to eat by himself to see what he does when he thinks he is unobserved. This might give you some helpful clues.

EATING PROFICIENCY GUIDELINES

Although the types of eating skills discussed in the previous section are fairly comprehensive, they are all alike in one way: The goal is to teach new skills or to increase the frequency of selected eating behaviors. However, with severely and profoundly handicapped students, eating difficulties may also involve (1) refusal to eat, (2) eating very sloppily or "pigging" food, or (3) throwing up food regularly. The guidelines provided here summarize what researchers in this area have done. Unfortunately, only a few published reports deal with these frustrating eating problems.

Refusal to Eat

Severely handicapped students only infrequently refuse to eat. However, one reason that they do is the overprotective nature of many parents and families with handicapped children. Failing to place normal behavioral requirements on children allows them to become dependent on the family. When others try to encourage independent eating, resistance by the child leads to an unpleasant eating period. There are at least three ways of attempting to cope with this difficulty:

1.   If parents are responsive and willing, begin to teach them how to develop self-feeding responses in their child.

2.   If the teacher must assume full responsibility, then selection of preferred foods and presentation of one preferred food at a time by a highly reinforcing person is desirable (e.g., Wehman & Marchant, 1978). When a predetermined goal is reached, such as 5 days in a row of accepting food, a second food can be used.

3.   Withholding food will lead to increased hunger and will break down the student's resistance to accept food. The obvious problem with this method is the ethical difficulty of depriving a child of food.

Sloppy Eating

Many severely handicapped children play with food, spill it excessively, throw it, and so on. These inappropriate eating responses can be eliminated and good eating can be trained. Below are several suggestions:

1.   Making the removal of the child's food immediately contingent on the sloppy eating behavior has worked repeatedly and is advised as one possibility. With this method the teacher should remove the food for about 10 to 30 seconds immediately after the last bit of food has been swallowed and tell the child why the food was removed.

2.   A second method is physical guidance of correct responses and then gradual removal of teacher assistance as the child becomes more proficient; preferred foods may be used as reinforcers for "good" eating.

3.   If the child persists in sloppy eating, a third strategy would be the combined use of:

A. preferred food as reinforcement for good eating, and

B. cleaning up the spilled food by rapidly guiding the child through the entire clean-up process of washing the floor, wringing out the cloth, and so on.

Chronic Regurgitation

Another eating behavior problem exhibited by severely and profoundly handicapped students is throwing up after every meal. This is usually done for the attention that it inevitably brings. No teacher cares to let vomitus lie on the floor, and it is a typical reaction to believe the child is physically ill, anxiety-ridden, or suffering from some emotional distress. However, if the child vomits regularly, it may be that the teacher's attention after each vomiting period is strengthening the vomiting behavior. There are two possible methods of overcoming this problem:

1. Give the child extra portions of food at meals until he will take no more. The rationale behind this is that many children bring up the food to experience the taste in their mouth, and complete food satiation at mealtime decreases this maladaptive response (Jackson, Johnson, Ackron, & Crowley, 1975).

2. If this strategy is not successful, a combination of two procedures can be used:

    A. Positive reinforcement and attention can be given for *not* vomiting.

    B. When the child does throw up, he should have to complete the entire clean-up very rapidly and with physical guidance (Azrin & Wesolowski, 1975).

Certainly, these methods are not all-inclusive or detailed. However they should give some indication of the possible methods that can be implemented. If there are doubts about how to utilize these methods, a professional consultant trained in behavior modification should be brought in.

DRESSING AND GROOMING SKILLS

There are a number of resources that specify the procedures necessary for the development of dressing and grooming behaviors in the severely and profoundly retarded (e.g., Anderson, Hodson, & Jones, 1975; Gardner, 1971; Myers, Sinco, & Stalma, 1974). Each of these sources provides instructional programs or guidelines for implementing dressing and grooming programs.

Several research studies directly examine instructional procedures involved in training children in dressing skills (Karen & Maxwell, 1967; Martin, Kehoe, Bird, Jensen, & Darbyshire, 1971; Minge & Ball, 1967). The Martin (1971) study is particularly helpful because it summarizes the number of sessions, minutes, average initial performance, and final performance information relating to the learning of dressing skills by severely retarded girls. Unfortunately, most of the dressing studies do not address the issue of the efficacy of forward versus backward chaining with an array of different dressing skills.

Personal hygiene has been taught the severely retarded by a variety of instructional techniques. Hand washing and face washing (Treffry, Martin, Samels & Watson, 1970) and tooth brushing (Horner & Keilitz, 1975) were taught through task analysis and positive reinforcement. Other grooming skills such as independent hair washing (Hamre, 1974) and using mouthwash (Nietupski, 1974) have been taught to children through imitation, illustrative pictures, and task analysis.

Table 2–3 analyzes studies that demonstrate the acquisition of dressing and grooming skills. The scheme used is similar to those used in Tables 2–1 and 2–2.

GENERAL DRESSING AND UNDRESSING GUIDELINES

Dressing skills are best taught in realistic situations such as toileting sessions, arriving at school, and preparing to leave school. It is also necessary to schedule weekly sessions in the classroom to work on dressing behaviors that need special attention or on skills that do not lend themselves to daily classroom activities. The following suggestions might be implemented during such sessions:

1. Each child should be assessed to determine which steps of a skill he is able to perform unassisted. A task analysis of each activity will help the teacher assess the child. Every person working in the classroom should be aware of what level of assistance each child needs so that no child is given more physical assistance than is required.
2. Undressing is usually easier for a child than dressing, so training should begin with this. Backward chaining is usually the best instructional technique to use with dressing since the child receives early satisfaction.
3. Several concrete suggestions for undressing and dressing instruction follow:

   A. Make sure the child's clothes are about two sizes too big so that they can be removed with ease.

Table 2–3. Dressing and Grooming Studies

Study	Sample size	Subject characteristics	Institutionalization	Research design	Teaching procedures	Response measure	Length of study or training time
Dressing							
Karen & Maxwell (1967) (Buttoning)	1	7-year-old boy	No	Clinical study; no control group	Positive reinforcement plus gradual reduction in button size	Numerical performance; rating, trials, and time in seconds	Not reported
Minge & Ball (1967)	6	Profound retardation; girls	Yes	Pre- to post-clinical study; no control group	Task analysis and food reinforcement	Number of dressing steps completed	57 days; two 15-minute sessions daily
Martin, Kehoe, Bird, Jensen, & Darbyshire (1971)	11	Severe/profound retardation; 7–20-year-old girls and women	Yes	AB	Positive reinforcement of individual components in dressing response chains; forward and backward chaining used	Scoring system of 1—independent 2—verbal prompt 3—partial physical help 4—complete physical help	Comprehensive time of session data available across five skills

Study	N	Population		Design	Treatment	Dependent measure	Duration
Ball, Seric, & Payne (1971)	6	Severe/profound retardation; 9–13-year-old boys	Yes	AB	Positive reinforcement of component skills in dressing chains		90 days
Ford (1975)	1	Profoundly retarded 8-year-old boy	No	Clinical study; no control group	Backward chaining plus food reinforcement	Percentage of correct responses in putting on shirt	16 sessions
Grooming/appearance							
Hunt, Fitzhugh, & Fitzhugh (1968) (cleanliness)	12	Moderately retarded; 12 men	Yes	Clinical study; no control group	Token reinforcement	Frequency of days of appropriate appearance during different reinforcement schedules	34 days
Hamilton, Allen, Stephano, & Davall (1969) (sanitary napkins)	76	Severe retardation; women, men, age 21	Yes	Two clinical studies comparing types of reinforcers and correction procedures	Positive reinforcement	Percentage of steps in task correct	9 months

Table 2-3. (Continued)

Study	Sample size	Subject characteristics	Institutionalization	Research design	Teaching procedures	Response measure	Length of study or training time
Treffry, Martin, Samuels, & Watson (1970) (grooming)	30	Severe retardation; girls	Yes	AB	Task analysis, fading of physical assistance, and 15-second time-outs for wrong responses	Number of steps completed in grooming program	9 weeks
Abramson & Wunderlich (1972) (tooth brushing)	9	Severely retarded males	Yes	Clinical study; trials to criterion	Social reinforcement plus two-choice discriminative learning	Trials to criterion	Not reported
Wehman (1974) (cleanliness)	15	Moderate/severe retardation; geriatric women	Yes	Clinical study; no control group	Token economy with stars posted on board	Number of stars earned for good grooming	60 days

50

Hamre (1974) (hair shampooing)	39	Moderate/severely retarded adolescents	No	Clinical study; pre-posttest and trials to criterion	Social reinforcement and task analysis format	Number of correct steps	Not reported
Nietupski (1974) (mouthwash)	7	Moderate/severely retarded adolescents	No	Clinical study; pre-posttest and trials to criterion	Social reinforcement and task analysis format	Percentage of correct responses	Not reported
Horner & Kelitz (1975) (tooth brushing)	8	Moderately retarded adolescents	Yes	Multiple baseline across individuals	Social and token reinforcement	Number of correct steps	40 sessions
Smeets, Bouter, & Bouter (1976) (tooth brushing)	4	Severe retardation; mean age, 25 years	Yes	Clinical study	Task analysis and forward chaining	Amount of assistance required at each step in task analysis	33 sessions

B. Use socks without heels (tube socks for children) in the first sessions. Backward chaining helps the child learn to manipulate the heel area effectively. When the child can pull this type sock on, introduce stretchy cotton blend socks with heels. Follow this with regular nylon socks.

C. To train children in putting on or removing crew-neck shirts, first teach the child to raise and lower a hula hoop or similar aid over the head. When the child has learned these hand motions, introduce a dressing shirt which has only a hole for the head. Have the child learn to raise and lower this over her head by modeling and physically assisting her. Then move on to an oversized T-shirt, followed by a shirt the child would normally wear. Some children will take a long time to learn removing the shirt over their head and then from the arms, so it is better to have them learn to pull their arms out before raising the shirt over their heads.

D. Putting on a coat is facilitated if the child is taught to lay the coat flat in front with the neck closest to the body. The child then places one arm in each sleeve, lifts both arms high to throw the coat over his head, and then pushes each arm on through the sleeve.

E. For practical purposes, when teaching a child to remove his coat, carry the instruction further to include picking it up and hanging it in the proper place in the classroom.

F. Buttoning is facilitated if the following steps are taken:

(1) Have the child learn to drop a wooden disk through a vertical and a horizontal opening in a box made of three pieces of wood.

(2) Have the child learn to pass the disk from one hand to another through the same slots.

(3) Repeat steps 1 and 2 using a large button and a piece of vinyl or leather.

(4) Use large buttons on regular material.

(5) Use smaller buttons and have them attached to material.

(6) Use the child's regular clothing or dressing jackets with buttons large enough for child to manipulate.

Individual Teaching Guidelines

The sequence presented below is directed to those teachers who must use one-to-one training. This may also be necessary because of staff limitations or because of the extreme handicap of the child.

1. How to prepare a teaching session

    A. *Room selection.* Select a room or area without distractions. Consider whether the curtains are pulled and toys are removed, and whether only you and child are there. The room should be quiet.

    B. *Position.* The position of child and teacher should be set up so that you are facing each other. Sit on a chair at the same level as the child so it is easy to reach him.

    C. *Materials and equipment.* Have clothing laid out, and reinforcers and record-keeping materials ready before you begin the training session.

D. *Time of day.* Be as consistent as possible in teaching the same time each day—perhaps in the morning, evening, or before and after naps.

E. *Length of sessions.* Length may vary, but an optimum time is about 15 to 20 minutes per session. It is better to teach for several short periods daily rather than in infrequent long sessions.

2. Techniques to consider using in a teaching session

The techniques listed below are ones that can be used with all levels of retarded children. Your skill in using reinforcers, fading, and shaping will help the child to learn.

A. *Reinforcing the skill you are teaching.* When the consequences of a child's responses increase the probability of its occurrence, they are called reinforcers.

B. *Kinds of reinforcers*
   (1) Teacher's social praise
      (A) If the child will learn with only your attention, this is the reinforcer to use.
      (B) Examples of social praise are smiling, eye contact, clapping hands, singing part of song, patting on the back, hugging, and making positive statements.
   (2) If you're using a food reinforcer, such as ice cream, it is more effective if it is limited to the teaching session only.

Other examples of food reinforcers are Sugar Pops, cakes, cookies, Coke, sandwiches, donuts, pretzels, or whatever food is a favorite of the child.

(3) Use small pieces of reinforcer.

(4) If the child appears to be losing interest or not making progress, check to see if he is tired of the reinforcer.

(5) If you use a food reinforcer, be sure to praise at the same time you give the reinforcer. Your goal is to use only social praise eventually, so you should pair food and social praise at first, then graudally decrease the food.

C. *How to use reinforcers*

1. Consistency

    (A) When the child is first learning a new skill, it is necessary to use social praise and/or food every time he achieves a step.

    (B) Later, when the child has acquired the skill, you can reinforce it every other time or less frequently.

2. Immediacy

    (A) In order for the child to know what dressing step you want, it is necessary to reinforce the child immediately after the performance of that step or approximation of the step.

D. *Shaping and fading.* These two important techniques are listed together because as the trainer shapes the dressing skill planned in the child, physical and verbal help should be simultaneously phased out. Remember, your goal is to have the child dress independently.

(1) Fading is the process of gradually removing your physical help as you see and feel the child taking over the dressing skill. For example, when you feel the child is beginning to pull up his pants, gradually decrease the amount of pulling you do, allowing him to become more and more independent.

(2) Shaping consists of reinforcing closer and closer approximations of the desired goal. Your dressing goal may be putting on a T-shirt independently, or one step in a particular method of putting on a T-shirt.

(3) How to use fading and shaping

    (A) You often begin teaching a step by putting your hand over the child's hand and physically putting him through the step.

    (B) As you feel him begin to take over, begin to fade out your physical assistance and praise the child's efforts.

    (C) As the child begins to approximate the step, the emphasis now should switch from your physical help to reinforcing the child for doing step on her own.

    (D) Once you have faded your physical help, you should begin to decrease the reinforcers gradually. The ultimate goal is to have the child dress himself with minimal cues.

Group Teaching Guidelines

A more realistic means of teaching is with two or more children. The points identified below indicate several considerations involved in training dressing skills to small groups of severely handicapped students.

1. When to use group teaching

    A. Group teaching is practical when the staff is too small or there is not enough time to check on detailed progress.
    B. Children can be grouped together for similar dressing skills such as putting on coats, hats, and mittens.

2. Considerations when teaching retarded children in a group

    A. Place children in chairs on their own level.
    B. The teacher should be able to move freely from child to child, for example, by using a chair on rollers.
    C. If children cannot imitate each other or the teacher, it is better to work with each child individually and to have the other children wait for their turn.
    D. It is better to work on only one dressing task at a time, such as the T-shirt. You may need more than one item of clothing, depending on the size and the abilities of your group.
    E. If the children do imitate, let the child who can do the most model for the other children.
    F. If the children have accomplished many of the tasks but need practice in the dressing skills, dress-up games can be played. If

dress-up clothing is used, check to make certain of three points:

(1)   The clothing must not be too big or too small.

(2)   Fastenings should be within reach of the children.

(3)   Fastenings should be large enough for the children to grasp and hold onto, such as buttons and zippers.

A mirror lets the child see his or her own accomplishments. Remember that mirrors do create a reverse image, so they are not effective in teaching, only as a reinforcer. Some children's behavior is affected by use of shiny objects.

G.   You may want to pair the group teaching session with:

(1)   The season
Jacket—winter
Mittens—snow
Sweater—fall, etc.

(2)   Activities of the day
Jackets and sweaters—field trips or recess
Shoes and socks—rest time, etc.

EVALUATION OF SELF-HELP PROGRAMS

Results of the studies reviewed in this chapter reveal some of the major advances made toward an instructional technology of self-help skill training. The first obvious positive feature of this analysis is the accumulation of empirical evidence over the past decade which supports the effectiveness of behavior modification as a means of developing self-help skills in the severely and profoundly mentally retarded. Secondly, it is apparent that instructional techniques and approaches to training different skills have become increasingly sophisticated in recent years; this is particularly evident in toileting and eating. Since the work of Azrin and his associates (1971; 1973; 1974), toilet training and eating procedures have become comprehensive in focus that is, *all* component skills are being taught. In addition, they have become more efficient in terms of training time required.

Although over 70 percent of the studies reviewed took place in institutional settings, this should change in future years as severely handicapped individuals are moved to group homes and public school classrooms. It may be anticipated that self-help skill training which takes place in classrooms will need follow-through by parents at home. Parents and family members must be trained in self-care training so that there will be a transfer of training from classroom to home.

Much of the research described in this analysis was not evaluated through experimental/control group designs or rigorous within-subject designs. Although reversal designs may not always be appropriate because of ethical or logistical constraints, the changing criterion design (Groves & Carroccio, 1971) and multiple baseline designs across behaviors (e.g., Barton et al., 1970; Kazdin, 1973) would give greater internal validity to studies. The frequent lack of experimental control and the small sample size in many reports are major drawbacks to evaluating much of the self-help skill research.

Although many of the studies reported brief follow-ups, planned transfer of training and response maintenance was not a feature of most studies. This is perhaps the greatest limitation of the voluminous amount of self-help skill literature. Training in many skills occurred in ward environments and with institutional materials (e.g., Wehman, Abramson, & Norman, 1977).

It should be evident from the analyses presented in Tables 2–1, 2–2, and 2–3 that task analysis, modeling, prompting and fading, and reinforcement are characteristic of most of the self-help skill programs reviewed. In the limited number of studies that omitted manual guidance and relied solely on modeling and demonstration (Nelson, Cone, & Hanson, 1975), results were not positive. Most behavior-shaping efforts require a combination of instruction, modeling by the trainer, and in many cases physical prompting.

Task analysis, or the breaking down of a behavior into smaller components, was critical in the learning process with the severely and profoundly handicapped (Knapczyk, 1975). Tables 2–4, 2–5, and 2–6 provide task analyses of dressing skills such as tooth brushing, putting on pants, and putting on a sweater. These task analyses illustrate how a self-help skill can be subdivided into many little steps.

Although a task analysis format of instruction with positive reinforcement given for each step has been effective, a word of caution should be given about implementing self-care programs. There are several points which, if neglected, may lead to failure. Unfortunately, these errors are not usually discussed in the reported research:

1. The skill may not have been subdivided into small enough steps.
2. Manual guidance may be removed too quickly or too slowly.
3. The skill may not be appropriate for the developmental level of the child, that is, readiness skills may be lacking.
4. The child may not have been trained in simple attending skills.
5. Reinforcement parameters such as amount, immediacy, and schedule of reinforcement may not have been effectively manipulated or controlled.
6. If food is being used as a reinforcer, the training

Table 2–4. Brushing Teeth

Steps:

1.   Remove toothbrush and toothpaste from cup.
2.   Unscrew toothpaste cap.
3.   Squeeze appropriate amount of toothpaste onto brush.
4.   Lay toothbrush down.
5.   Screw cap back on tube.
6.   Pick up brush in preferred hand.
7.   Lean over sink.
8.   Brush in down motion over top teeth from one side of mouth to the other.
9.   Spit out excess at least once.
10. Brush in up motion over bottom teeth from one side of mouth to the other.
11. Spit out excess at least once.
12. Brush in down motion over back of top teeth from one side of mouth to the other.
13. Spit out excess at least once.
14. Brush in up motion over back of bottom teeth from one side of mouth to the other.
15. Spit out excess at least once.
16. Brush back and forth over crowns of top teeth from one side of mouth to the other.
17. Spit out excess at least once.
18. Brush back and forth over crowns of bottom teeth from one side of mouth to the other.
19. Spit out excess at least once.
20. Pick up cup.
21. Turn on cold water faucet.
22. Fill cup with water.
23. Rinse mouth with water.
24. Spit out excess at least once.
25. Pour excess water out of cup into sink.
26. Replace cup next to sink.
27. Rinse toothbrush in water.
28. Turn off cold water faucet.
29. Replace brush and paste in cup.

Table 2–5. Putting on and Tying a Pair of Shoes

Behavioral objective: Given a pair of tie shoes, the child will independently put them on and tie them eight out of ten times.

Task analysis:

1. Pick up left shoe.
2. Place left shoe on floor in front of left foot.
3. Grasp sides of shoe with both hands.
4. Pull sides of shoe outward.
5. Hold tongue of shoe with left hand.
6. Place foot in shoe.
7. Pull tongue up and straight.
8. Hold one lace by end in one hand.
9. Pull laces straight.
10. Let go of laces.
11. With index finger and thumb of both hands, grasp each lace in the middle.
12. Cross laces.
13. Put right lace into left hand.
14. Put left lace into right hand.
15. Pull laces straight.
16. Place index finger of left hand where laces cross.
17. Grasp right lace with index finger of right hand.
18. Push lace through hole.
19. Pull laces straight and tight.
20. Let go of right lace.
21. Place index finger and thumb in middle of left lace.
22. Pull upper part of lace down, forming loop.
23. Pick up right lace with right hand.
24. Bring right lace around to front of loop.
25. Push right lace through hole under loop with thumb.
26. With left hand pull right lace through hole forming another loop.
27. Grasp right loop with right hand.
28. Grasp left loop with left hand.
29. Pull laces tight, keeping both loops in place.
30. Repeat steps 1–29 with right shoe.

Table 2-6 Putting on a Pair of Pants

Behavioral objective: The student will successfully put on a pair of pants, zip, and snap them within 5 minutes at least eight out of ten times.

Task analysis:

1. Grasp top of pants with both hands.
2. Hold pants in front of stomach.
3. Turn pants until zipper of pants is the part farthest from stomach.
4. With left hand, hold onto pants at left side of snap.
5. With right hand, hold onto pants at right side of snap.
6. Sit down.
7. Bend body over at waist.
8. Hold pants in front of legs at calf level.
9. Raise right foot.
10. Move foot over back of pants toward front.
11. Point toes of right foot.
12. Place right foot into inside of pants.
13. With toe pointed, slide right foot into top of right leg hole.
14. Extend right leg through right pants leg opening.
15. Place right hand below knee on right pants leg.
16. Pull right pants leg up.
17. Pull pants leg up until bottom of right pants leg is at right ankle.
18. Put foot down.
19. Let go of pants leg.
20. With right hand, hold onto front of pants at right side of snap.
21. Raise left foot up.
22. Raise left foot over back of pants.
23. Point toes of left foot.
24. Place left foot into inside of pants.
25. With toes pointed, slide left foot into top of left leg opening.
26. Extend left leg through left pants leg opening.
27. Place left hand below knee on left pants leg.
28. Pull left pants leg up.
29. Pull pants leg up until bottom of left pants leg is at left ankle.
30. Let go of pants leg.
31. Put left foot down.
32. Stand up.

Table 2–6.   (Continued)

33. Place left hand on top of left side of pants.
34. Place right hand on top of right side of pants.
35. Grasp pants with both hands.
36. Pull pants up.
37. Pull pants up until over bottom.
38. Let go of pants.
39. Place left hand at top of pants in on left side.
40. Hold top of pants.
41. Place thumb and forefinger of right hand at bottom of zipper.
42. Grasp zipper tab of zipper with fingers.
43. Pull zipper tab of zipper up.
44. Pull zipper tab of zipper until it reaches top of pants.
45. Let go of zipper tab.
46. With right hand, touch snap on right side of pants.
47. Place left hand on snap at left side of pants.
48. With left hand, grasp pants at left side of snap.
49. With right hand, place right snap on top of left snap.
50. With right hand, place forefinger on top of snap.
51. Place thumb underneath bottom of snap.
52. Press fingers together tightly until snaps faster to each other.
53. Let go of pants.

may proceed before the food is completely consumed.

7. The child may not be attending at the beginning of each trial.

8. The child may not have been given enough practice or allowed enough trials to learn the skill.

With an understanding of behavior-shaping techniques and attention to some of the above-mentioned pitfalls in programming, teachers should be able to train severely handicapped students to be independent in self-care skills. The results of previous research synthesized here should allow the teacher unfamiliar with the severely and profoundly handicapped to compare and evaluate her efforts with those of others working in the field.

REFERENCES

Abramson, E., & Wunderlich, R. Dental hygiene training for retardates. An application of behavioral techniques. *Mental Retardation,* 1972, *10,* 6–8.

Anderson, D., Hodson, G., & Jones, W. *Instructional programs for handicapped students.* Springfield, Illinois: Charles C. Thomas, 1975.

Azrin, N. H., & Armstrong, P. The "mini-meal"—A method for teaching eating skills to the profoundly retarded. *Mental Retardation,* 1973, *11,* 9–13.

Azrin, N. H., & Foxx, R. A rapid method of toilet training the institutionalized retarded. *Journal of Applied Behavior Analysis,* 1971, *4,* 89–99.

Azrin, N. H., Sneed, T., & Foxx, R. A rapid method of eliminating bed-wetting (enuresis) of the retarded. *Behavior Research and Therapy,* 1973, *11,* 427–434.

Azrin, N. H., Sneed, T., & Foxx, R. Dry bed training: Rapid elimination of childhood enuresis. *Behavior Research and Therapy,* 1974, *12,* 147–156.

Azrin, N. H., & Wesolowski, M. Eliminating habitual vomiting in a retarded adult by positive practice and self-correction. *Journal of Behavior Therapy and Experimental Psychiatry,* 1975, *6(2),* 145–148.

Ball, T., Seric, K., & Payne L. Long-term retention of self-help skill training in the profoundly retarded. *American Journal of Mental Deficiency,* 1971, *76,* 378–382.

Barton, F. S., Guess, D., Garcia, E., & Baer, D. Improvement of retardates' mealtime behaviors by time-out procedures using multiple baseline techniques. *Journal of Applied Behavior Analysis,* 1970, *3,* 77–84.

Baumeister, A., & Klosowski, R. An attempt to group toilet train severely retarded patients. *Mental Retardation,* 1965, *3,* 24–26.

Berkowitz, S., Sherry, P., & Davis, B. Teaching self-feeding skills to profound retardates using reinforcement and fading procedures. *Behavior Therapy,* 1971, *2,* 62–67.

Christian, W., Holloman, S., & Lanier, C. L. An attendant operated feeding program for severely and profoundly retarded females. *Mental Retardation,* 1973, *11,* 35–37.

Dayan, M. Toilet training retarded children in a state residential institution. *Mental Retardation,* 1964, *2,* 116–117.

Doleys, D., & Arnold, S. Treatment of childhood encopresis: Full cleanliness training. *Mental Retardation,* 1975, *13,* 14–16.

Eaton, P., & Brown, R. The training of mealtime behaviors in the subnormal. *British Journal of Mental Subnormality*, 1974, *20*, 78–85.

Ellis, N. R. Toilet training the severely defective patient: A stimulus response reinforcement. *American Journal of Mental Deficiency*, 1963, *68*.

Ford, L. Teaching dressing skills to a severely retarded child. *American Journal of Occupational Therapy*, 1975, *29*, 87–92.

Foxx, R., & Azrin, N. H. *Toilet training the retarded*. Champaign, Illinois: Research Press, 1973.

Gardner, W. I. *Behavior modification in mental retardation*. Chicago: Aldine-Atherton, 1971.

Gelbert, H. and Myer, V. Behavior therapy and encopresis: the complexities involved in treatment. *Behavior Research and Therapy*, 1965, *2*, 227–231.

Giles, D., & Wolf, M. M. Toilet training institutionalized severe retardates: An application of operant behavior modification techniques. *American Journal of Mental Deficiency*, 1966, *70(5)*, 761–780.

Gilhool, T. Changing public policies in the individualization of instruction: Roots and forces. *Education and Training of the Mentally Retarded*, 1976, *11*, 180–188.

Groves, I., & Carroccio, D. A self-feeding program for the severely and profoundly retarded. *Mental Retardation*, 1971, *9*, 10–11.

Hamilton, J., Allen, P., Stephano, L., & Davall, E. Training mentally retarded females to use sanitary napkins. *Mental Retardation*, 1969, *7*, 40–43.

Hamre, S. Family life curriculum. In L. Brown, W. Williams, & T. Crowner (Eds.), *A collection of papers and programs related to public school services for severely handicapped students* (Vol. 4). Madison, Wisconsin: Madison Public School System, 1974.

Henrikson, K., & Doughty, R. Decelerating undesirable mealtime behavior in a group of profoundly retarded boys. *American Journal of Mental Deficiency*, 1967, *72*, 42–44.

Horner, R. D., & Keilitz, I. Training mentally retarded adolescents to brush their teeth. *Journal of Applied Behavior Analysis*, 1975, *8*, 301–310.

Hundziak, M., Maurer, R., & Watson, L. Operant conditioning in toilet training of severely retarded boys. *American Journal of Mental Deficiency*, 1968, *70*, 120–125.

Hunt, J., Fitzhugh, L., & Fitzhugh, K. Teaching "exit-ward" patients appropriate personal appearance behavior by using reinforcement techniques. *American Journal of Mental Deficiency*, 1968, *73*, 41–48.

Jackson, G., Johnson, C., Ackron, G., & Crowley, R. Food satiation as a procedure to decelerate vomiting. *American Journal of Mental Deficiency*, 1975, *80*, 223–227.

Karen, R., & Maxwell, S. Strengthening self-help behavior in the retardate. *American Journal of Mental Deficiency*, 1967, *71*, 516–550.

Kazdin, A. E. Methodological and assessment considerations in evaluating reinforcement programs in applied settings. *Journal of Applied Behavior Analysis*, 1973, *78*, 134–140.

Kimbrell, D., Luckey, R., Barbuto, K., & Love, R. Institutional environment developed for training severely and profoundly retarded. *Mental Retardation*, 1967, *5*, 34–37.

Knapczyk, D. Task analytic assessment of severe learning problems. *Education and Training of the Mentally Retarded*, 1975, *10*, 74–77.

Levine, M., & Elliot, C. B. Toilet training for profoundly retarded with limited staff. *Mental Retardation*, 1970, *8*, 48–50.

Madsen, C., Madsen, C., & Thompson, F. Increasing rural Head Start children's consumption of middle class meals. *Journal of Applied Behavior Analysis*, 1974, *7*, 257–262.

Mahoney, K., Van Wagenen, R., & Meyerson, L. Toilet training of normal and retarded children. *Journal of Applied Behavior Analysis*, 1971, *4*, 173–182.

Martin, G., Kehoe, G., Bird, E., Jensen, V., & Darbyshire, M. Operant conditioning of dressing behavior in severely retarded girls. *Mental Retardation*, 1971. *9*, 27–30.

Martin, G., McDonald, S., & Ominchinski, M. An operant analysis of response interactions during meals with severely retarded girls. *American Journal of Mental Deficiency*, 1971, *75*, 68–75.

Minge, M., & Ball, T. Teaching of self-help skills to profoundly retarded patients. *American Journal of Mental Deficiency*, 1967, *71*, 864–868.

Myers, D., Sinco, R., & Stalma, M. *The right-to-education child.* Springfield, Illinois: Charles C. Thomas, 1974.

Nelson, G., Cone, J., & Hanson, C. Training correct utensil use in retarded children: Modeling versus physical guidance. *American Journal of Mental Deficiency*, 1975, *80*, 114–122.

Nietupski, J. Use of mouthwash. In L. Brown, W. Williams, & T. Crowner (Eds.), *A collection of papers and programs related to public school services for severely handicapped students* (Vol. 4). Madison, Wisconsin: Madison Public Schools, 1974.

O'Brien, F., & Azrin, N. H. Developing proper mealtime behaviors of the institutionalized retarded. *Journal of Applied Behavior Analysis*, 1972, *5*, 389–399.

O'Brien, F., Bugle, C., & Azrin, N. H. Training and maintaining a retarded child's proper eating. *Journal of Applied Behavior Analysis,* 1972, *5,* 67–72.

Osarchuk, M. Operant methods of toilet training of the severely and profoundly retarded: A review. *Journal of Special Education,* 1973, *7,* 423–437.

Rentfrow, R., & Rentfrow, D. Studies related to toilet training of the mentally retarded. *American Journal of Occupational Therapy,* 1969, *23,* 425–430.

Smeets, P., Bouter, R., & Bouter, H. Teaching toothbrushing behavior in severely retarded adults: A replication study. *British Journal on Mental Subnormality,* 1976, *22,* 5–12.

Smith, P., Britton, P., Johnson, M., & Thomas, D. Problems involved in toilet training profoundly mentally handicapped adults. *Behavior Research and Therapy,* 1975, *15,* 301–307.

Song, A., & Gandhi, R. An analysis of behavior during the acquisition and maintenance phase of self-spoon feeding skills of profound retardates. *Mental Retardation,* 1974, *12(1),* 25–28.

Stoltz, S., & Wolf, M. M. Visually discriminated behavior in a "blind" adolescent retardate. *Journal of Applied Behavior Analysis,* 1969, *2,* 65–77.

Treffry, D., Martin, G., Samuels, J., & Watson, O. Operant conditioning grooming behavior of severely retarded girls. *Mental Retardation,* 1970, *8,* 29–33.

Wehman, P. Maintaining oral hygiene skills in geriatric retarded women. *Mental Retardation,* 1974, *12,* 20.

Wehman, P., Abramson, M., & Norman, C. Transfer of training in behavior modification programs: An evaluative review. *Journal of Special Education,* 1977, *11(2),* 217–231.

Wehman, P., & Marchant, J. Reducing multiple problem behaviors of a profoundly handicapped child. *British Journal of Social and Clinical Psychology,* 1978.

Zeiler, M., & Jervey, S. S. Development of behavior: Self-feeding. *Journal of Consulting and Clinical Psychology,* 1968, *32,* 164–168.

Chapter 3

RECREATIONAL SKILL
DEVELOPMENT

Educational programs that emphasize the development of recreational and leisure-time skills in severely and profoundly handicapped students are receiving increased attention by special educators (Wehman, 1977a). Development of a leisure skill repertoire in students with severe behavioral handicaps may facilitate increased proficiency in language, motor skills, cognition, and social interaction (Strain, Cooke, & Apolloni, 1976). Furthermore, games and related recreational activities that are integrated into other areas of instructional programming provide functional tasks conducive to the establishment of a positive learning environment (e.g., Thiagarajan, 1976).

Unfortunately there are many difficulties in developing effective recreation programs for the severely mentally handicapped. Previous reviews of the literature (Wehman, 1977a; Hamre-Nietupski & Williams, 1976) have indicated at least four limitations and gaps in knowledge. One problem is the restricted age of the individuals who have generally participated in recreation training programs. Children and preschoolers receive the most attention, whereas adolescents and adults are only infrequently studied.

Secondly, the definition of leisure-time activity in research studies has been limited. Many recreation studies with the severely retarded have examined only one or two skills, such as ball rolling (Kazdin & Erickson, 1975; Morris & Dolker, 1974). The development of a more expanded repertoire of leisure skills in the same person has received limited study.

Selection of durable and age-appropriate toys is another problem that has plagued those involved in recreation program development for the severely handicapped (Wehman, 1976a). Innovative leisure-time materials for physically mature yet developmentally young retarded individuals are in limited supply.

The inability to identify the specific role that different instructional procedures have on leisure-time activity has also been an impediment to the development of replicable leisure-time programs. Cooke and Apolloni (1976) noted that most training in the area of social-emotional education combines instructions, modeling, manual guidance, and external reinforcement contingencies.

This chapter presents assessment techniques and instructional procedures that can be used to facilitate isolative play, cooperative play, and games and structured recreational activities. A series of task analyses and gross motor recreational programs are also presented. In an effort to avoid definitional problems the terms leisure time activity, recreation, and play are used interchangeably. In this chapter, free play may be considered as any action or combination of actions on objects which the child engages in for the apparent purpose of fun. These actions should not be harmful or destructive. Structured recreation is considered the goal-oriented and purposeful acquisition of a selected leisure skill such as riding a tricycle.

Developing Free Play Skills

Assessment: Use of Developmental Norms

When developing new skills in severely and profoundly handicapped persons, it is most desirable to provide a sequential hierarchy of responses which leads to a terminal objective (Gardner, 1974; White & Liberty, 1976). Skill sequencing can be applied to most programming areas, and can be developed through a logical task analysis or through an empirically verifiable behavior sequence. It is important that those involved in recreation programming for severely handicapped persons are cognizant of the developmental levels of play behavior that have been established with a nonretarded population of children. Although one must be cautious about making analogies between the behavior of nonretarded children and that of brain-damaged persons of similar mental ages, such a developmental sequence can provide guidelines and direction for arranging recreation environments.

Theoretical and empirical support has been given to the assumption that the social behavior exhibited in free play is developmental in nature. Gesell (1940) observed that the play of children followed a definite sequence through ages 1 to 5, moving from simple motor activities to socialized play. Parten (1932) observed the indoor play of 42 nonretarded preschool children ranging in age from 2 to 5. The observational scale was based on the degree of social participation required, and it included the following categories: unoccupied behavior, solitary play, onlooker behavior, parallel play, associative play, and cooperative play. Parten's data support a developmental sequence in that a definite relationship was found between age and degree of social participation. Almost 40 years later, Barnes (1971) performed a replication study with preschoolers. Results were highly similar to Parten's work with preschoolers, and thus further supported the validity of a developmental sequence of play.

Another analysis of developmental norms of leisure activity involving isolative play was the research performed by Tilton and Ottinger (1964). These workers compared the toy play of nonretarded young children, autistic children, and trainable retarded children. Play behavior was observed over a number of 20-minute sessions in a roomful of toys. Toys included building blocks, a tea set, a doll and doll clothes, a dump truck, a small wooden train, a pegboard and hammer, and a large stuffed bear. The greatest utility of this research was the attempt to sequence toy play behavior developmentally. The following hierarchy was advanced as a result of direct observation:

1. Repetitive manual manipulations
2. Oral contacts
3. Pounding with toys
4. Throwing toys
5. Pushing or pulling
6. Personalized uses of toys
7. Manipulations of movable part of toys
8. Separation of parts of toys
9. Combinational uses of toys

Complete descriptions of each category can be found in the report of Tilton and Ottinger (1964). The conclusion of this observational analysis was that children labeled "autistic" were lowest in the hierarchy of toy play skills that the retarded children next, and that the nonhandicapped children had the highest skills.

Careful examination of developmental norms of play facilitate assessment and evaluation in program development. In determining an appropriate point for initiating a free play program for severely and profoundly handicapped persons, it is necessary to observe the level of play activity (e.g., solitary, onlooker, or cooperative). From this assessment, instructional procedures and environmental arrangements can then be designed to promote greater development of recreational skills.

One assessment strategy that may be useful in determining when to initiate programming is to observe directly the type of free play with toys exhibited by students, and then to arrange the recreation environment accordingly. This hierarchy may be most effective if it is implemented with a fine-motor program. Clearly, this sequence of independent play development also corresponds to the development of rudimentary fine-motor skills in young children (Hurlock, 1972).

Assessment: A Clinical Perspective

The free play of severely and profoundly handicapped individuals may also be assessed by examining a different set of variables which characterize leisure activity. Instead of analyzing specific toy actions, as recommended by Tilton and Ottinger (1964), a behavioral analysis of the individuals' play skills can be made, also through direct observation. Several of these parameters are delineated below.

STIMULUS CONDITIONS OF PLAY SESSION.   In a functional analysis of behavior, it is essential to identify the stimulus conditions that are controlling the behavior (Gardner, 1971). The issue of stimulus control is crucial in the following questions: (1) do playful actions occur under the control of play materials presented in the environment? or (2) does play occur only under a verbal cue of an intervening teacher, or through viewing a more sophisticated peer model? Spontaneous free play can only occur when stimulus control is transferred from teacher cues to play materials. Previous research with play and retarded persons has examined how a teacher may acquire stimulus control over the individual (e.g., Redd, 1969). However little research effectively demonstrates a successful transfer of stimulus control from teacher prompts to presentation of play materials (Hopper & Wambold, in press).

ACTION ON PLAY MATERIALS.   When presented with toys or play objects, what does the individual do? He or she may sit, rock, shake them repetitively, destroy them, or totally ignore them, particularly if the individual is severely handicapped. The person may not have been sufficiently exposed to the potentially reinforcing qualities of different toys. Hence prompting appropriate actions with play materials can serve two functions: (1) It can set the occasion for the teacher to socially reinforce play behaviors, and (2) it can provide an opportunity to utilize toys in a reinforcer sampling procedure. Action on play objects may be operationally defined as touching, grasping, holding, or exploring.

RANGE OF PLAY MATERIALS.   Another logical variable to assess is the number of different play materials that are acted on. Acting only on the same one or two objects might be classified as repetitive or stereotypic if the materials do not lend themselves to the development of creative behavior, as does clay formation or block design, for example. The focus of this variable is to provide a concrete assessment of the child's curiosity or exploratory behavior.

TOY PREFERENCE.   Data from the previous two variables could also be used to determine if there was a preference for any toys or type of toy. Reactive toys (toys that are not static when acted upon) would appear to be the most satisfactory because they tend to meet general guidelines for maintaining arousal and interest through stimulus uncertainty, i.e., complexity, novelty, and dissonance (Ellis, 1973). Other helpful information includes how often certain toys are played with by the student. This might be helpful in choosing reinforcers and maximizing the use of different toys as potential reinforcers at a later time.

DURATION OF PLAY.   A behavioral assessment of play should also take into consideration the time spent playing. Many severely handicapped persons act appropriately on an assortment of materials, but only for a very brief period. Frequently, more prevalent behaviors include repetitive pacing, self-stimulating, or staring blankly throughout the recreation session. For a fuller picture of the individual's leisure activity patterns, data should be collected on the time spent engaging in play.

During recreation periods, it might be advisable to use materials that may encourage many different responses, such as different block formations (Goetz & Baer, 1973).

COOPERATIVE INTERACTION.   More advanced play skills are usually characterized by cooperative social interaction between peers. In many play situations, the student may be alone or only with a teacher. For a thorough evaluation of play skills, it is important to observe the individual with his or her peers. Factors to consider in assessing social interactions include how often the student initiates interactions, how the student responds to interactions directed toward him or her, and the general quality of the interactions (Hamre-Nietupski & Williams, 1976).

The assessment factors that have been described are not meant to be exhaustive, but rather indicative of the types of variables which may be considered before initiating instruction on recreational skills. It is necessary to observe directly how a student uses leisure activity when confronted with a roomful of toys, play materials, or novel objects. From this informal assessment, specific play behaviors can then be measured. For the most reliable information concerning leisure skills, it is advisable to collect several days of baseline data before beginning instruction or making some alteration in the recreation environment. The reason for this is that the play materials may be new to the students and they may be responding only to the novelty of the toys.

Before leaving this discussion on assessment of leisure skills, a final and far less comprehensive strategy for evaluating students' play behaviors should be mentioned. Those who do not wish to gather the specific types of information discussed above may want to consider using a more simple assessment method of autistic-isolative-cooperative play (Wehman & Marchant, 1978).

With this strategy, the teacher clearly defines the types of behaviors that are characteristic of these three basic developmental levels of play. For example, in the autistic play stage, characteristic behaviors might include not touching or physically acting on any play materials or nonfunctional repetitive actions for long periods of time. Isolative play might be considered as any appropriate behavior exhibited alone or away from other peers. Cooperative or social play would be the next level in the basic developmental sequence and would include such skills as physical or verbal interaction with other peers and teachers (Paloutzian, Hasazi, Streifel, & Edgar, 1971).

This assessment strategy is convenient and takes little time; it also makes collecting fairly accurate information easier because the categories are so broad and therefore easy to discriminate. However, this type of behavioral assessment does not capture many of the collateral skills that are clearly associated with play skill development, such as fine-motor skills, changes in emotionality, and social behavior.

Instructional Technology: Arranging the Recreation Environment

Once target behaviors are identified and assessed, training strategies and procedures must be chosen. As a general instructional model is provided by the continuum in Figure 3–1, which describes a sequence of training that may be followed in developing recreational skills with the severely handicapped. One goal of this sequence is to emphasize that different students require varied degrees of instruction.

The more proficient student may play appropriately with little assistance or supervision, and require only periodic variations in play materials. Other students may require a musical background (Zine, Ferolo, Hass, & Hass, 1975) or certain types of play materials (Favell & Cannon, 1977; Quilitch & Risley, 1973) before engaging in sustained play. Frequently, however, severely and profoundly handicapped individuals must have individualized assistance and instruction which leads them through a sequence of simple and consistent instructions, verbal prompting, modeling, and even physical guidance. The less able a student is to initiate play independently, the more instructional supervision is required by the teacher.

In this section, several techniques and procedures are discussed which may facilitate the acquisition of free play skills. The organization of this section involves, first, methods of arranging the recreation environment (e.g., antecedent stimulus conditions) and, second, procedures that can be classified as consequences of leisure-time activity.

ANTECEDENT CONDITIONS.   Different materials, instructions, types of models, and toy arrangements are among the types of antecedent conditions that may facilitate leisure-time activity. An advantage to judicious arrangement of the recreation environment is that play may be more

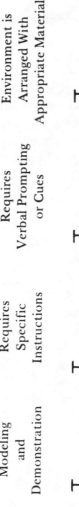

Requires Physical Guidance

Requires Modeling and Demonstration

Requires Specific Instructions

Requires Verbal Prompting or Cues

Responds when Environment is Arranged With Appropriate Materials

Figure 3–1. An instructional sequence for developing play skills.

spontaneous and not under the control of artificial reinforcers such as food.

Toy Proximity. One factor that may contribute to the development of increased leisure-time activity is the proximity of
recreation materials to participants in the program. Strate-
gic placement of several materials near a student may elicit
greater activity and allow for greater spontaneity in recreation sessions. Several reports stress the critical aspects of
ecological arrangement and space utilization (Cataldo &
Risley, 1974; Twardosz, Cataldo, & Risley, 1974).

Recent research indicates that proximity of toys to profoundly retarded adolescents and adults increased physical
action on objects from a mean baseline level of approximately 20 percent to almost 70 percent (Wehman, 1978).
This intervention consisted of having an adult place two
different toys near individuals who did not play appropriately. The toys were left near them for 30 consecutive seconds. Figure 3–2 displays the effects of toy proximity on the
mean percentage of action on objects exhibited by the
three students. In this study, the effects of modeling and
instructions plus modeling were also examined.

The effects of toy proximity could best be examined in
future research by eliminating the teachers and gradually
expanding the size of the recreation setting from very small
to a normal size playroom. Placing many toys near students
would be a logical derivative of a play environment which
was initially very small. As exploratory activity was increased through the sampling of different toys, the environment could gradually be expanded. This strategy could
easily be adapted in classrooms with bookshelves and other
room dividers. Furthermore, it would minimize the need
for extra adults and allow for spontaneous play.

Selecting Play Materials. The play materials are a critical feature of recreation environments for both retarded and
nonretarded children. The specific problems in selection of
appropriate toys and suggestions for overcoming these

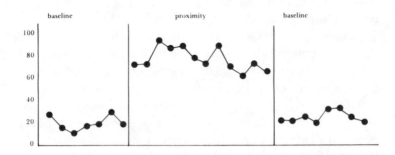

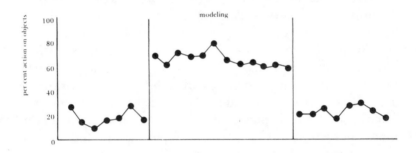

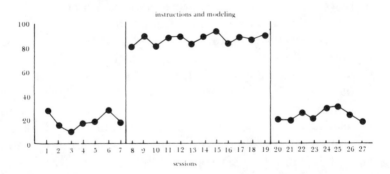

Figure 3–2. Mean percentage of action on objects by
three students under experimental conditions of toy
proximity, modeling, and instructions plus modeling.

difficulties have been discussed previously (Wehman, 1976a). Many of the recommended play material guidelines were based on the experimental research performed by child psychologists with nonhandicapped infants and pre-schoolers (e.g., McCall, 1974). Although there is little doubt that reactive materials influence exploratory actions or that socially oriented materials such as table games (Qui-litch & Risley, 1973) influence the level of social interactions, greater attention must be given to empirically verifying the effectiveness of different materials with the severely and profoundly handicapped.

Favell and Cannon (1977) recently evaluated 20 different toys with institutionalized, severely retarded females and found little relationship between toy preference and price. They found that different subjects showed strong preferences for different toys. For the most part, the preferred materials were reactive in nature.

Some support may be given to the value of balls, paddleballs, bubbleblowers, Lincoln Logs, and viewmasters with severely handicapped students (Wehman, 1978; Williams, Pumpian, McDaniel, Hamre-Nietupski, & Wheeler, 1975). Table 3–1 displays the rank order preferences of play materials that were acted on across 50 training and baseline sessions by three profoundly handicapped individuals (Wehman, in press). Unfortunately, these findings are confounded by the lack of control of toy selection. Each teacher was instructed to select different leisure-time materials and to present them according to the guidelines given in each experimental condition. However, no provision was made for collecting data on which materials were presented to which individuals most frequently.

It seems safe to say at this point that reactive materials may be the most effective in eliciting movement from nonambulatory or multiply handicapped students and, in general, may facilitate isolative play. However, more research is needed to learn how materials with different

Table 3–1   Toy Preferences Across Clients

Rank-ordered toy preference	Percentages collapsed across conditions
1. Lincoln Logs	54.2%
2. Balls	48.3%
3. Paddleball	41.3%
4. Bubble blower	27.3%
5. Coloring book	18.2%
6. Marble shaker	13.4%
7. Movie viewer	12.5%
8. Bowling kit	9.1%
9. Yo-yo	9.1%
10. Slinkies	8.2%
11. Life preserver	7.7%
12. Hockey game	7.2%
13. Silly String	6.9%
14. Music box	6.9%
15. Frisbee	5.6%
16. Scooters	5.3%
17. Pinball machine	4.0%

stimulus characteristics (e.g., plasticity, sound potential) affect the leisure activity of severely and profoundly handicapped persons.

Instructions. Verbal cues and instructions as antecedent stimulus conditions may also be a factor in encouraging more leisure-time activity, promoting social play, and teaching games that require rules. Instructions have been consistently influential in the behavior development of the developmentally disabled (Cooke & Apolloni, 1976; Kazdin, Silverman, & Sittler, 1975). When instructions have been paired with the modeling of appropriate leisure-time activity (Wehman, 1977b) or with appropriate social behavior such as smiling or saying hello (Nelson, Gibson, & Cutting, 1973; Gibson, Lawrence, & Nelson, 1977), the target behavior has been learned quickly. Instructions should be .

given consistently and with a minimum of extraneous language cues.

In a recent study which I performed with Jo Ann Marchant, instructions and modeling were given to a class of severely and profoundly handicapped children to improve their free play skills (Wehman & Marchant, 1977). Autistic, isolative, and cooperative play skill levels were assessed and measured during play sessions each day. By employing an ABAB reversal design, we were able to evaluate the effects of instructions and teacher modeling on the different levels of free play. Although teacher instruction decreased the amount of autistic play in each child, the most significant result was the substantial increase in cooperative play during instructional periods. This effect was noted in each child. Table 3–2 summarizes the data for each child and across conditions.

Table 3–2. Mean Percentage of Play

	Baseline	Treatment	Baseline	Treatment
Risa				
Autistic	34.0	7.7	53.3	10.0
Isolative	39.0	45.2	38.0	63.0
Cooperative	27.0	47.1	8.7	27.0
Larry				
Autistic	40.0	20.7	20.0	18.0
Isolative	60.0	32.3	80.0	62.0
Cooperative	0	47.0	0	20.0
Mack				
Autistic	83.0	42.6	64.0	45.0
Isolative	17.0	24.0	36.0	43.0
Cooperative	0	33.4	0	12.0
Rosemary				
Autistic	7.0	13.3	5.0	32.0
Isolative	93.0	46.3	95.0	42.0
Cooperative	0	40.4	0	26.0

Modeling. Specific effects of modeling in play sessions have not been closely examined and bear greater investigation. The influential role of modeling is well documented with a nonretarded population (e.g., Bandura, 1969), as it is with the mentally retarded (Baer, Peterson, & Sherman, 1967; Gibson et al., 1977; Wehman, 1976b). The positive implications of integrating retarded children into physical education and recreation classes with non-handicapped children may well be realized if the environment is carefully arranged (Snyder, Cooke, & Apolloni, 1977).

Some attempts at pairing higher-functioning peer models and adult models with severely and profoundly handicapped individuals have been successful in developing social play (Morris & Dolker, 1974; Kazdin & Erickson, 1975) and independent play (Paloutzian et al., 1971; Wehman, 1977b; Wehman & Marchant, 1977; 1978; Wehman, Karan, & Rettie, 1976). Nonretarded 8-year-olds have also been integrated into a playroom with trainable retarded children and encouraged to interact with each other through cooperative play (Knapczyk & Peterson, 1975). It was discovered that cooperative play increased substantially in the trainable retarded children when nonretarded 8-year-olds were present. These results were evaluated in a reversal design and indicated that, contingent on the removal of these models, cooperative play levels decreased to baseline rates.

Physical Prompting and Fading. Severely handicapped individuals frequently do not follow instructions because of non-compliance or failure to understand commands. When this happens in a learning situation, teachers are faced with the problem of how to elicit a desired behavior, or a component response in a behavior chain. If the behavior is not demonstrated, there is little opportunity for reinforcement (Whaley & Malott, 1971). Only when the desired response occurs and is followed with positive reinforcement can the behavior become stronger.

When developing new recreation skills in severely and profoundly handicapped students, a teacher may have to physically guide the individual through the desired skill or response (Whitman, Mercurio, & Caponigri, 1970). To encourage a profoundly handicapped child to pull a wagon or roll a ball, the teacher may have to guide the child manually, providing praise and affection contingent on successful approximations of the behavior.

Fading requires gradual removal of the physical guidance that is initially given in development of the skill. Timing the removal of the physical prompts is an art which a competent teacher gains only with experience. No amount of didactic instruction or lecture can replace the practical experience of prompting and fading. The importance of when to fade is critical. Removal of physical prompts too early or before the behavior is well established results in loss of that behavior and thus requires that the response sequence be started over again. Failure to fade a prompt, on the other hand, often leads to dependence on the trainer. Excessive use of prompts may result in a lack of self-initiated behavior by students.

Physical prompting is recommended only when all other efforts at arranging the play environment have failed. By manually putting the student through target responses, a great deal of fun may be taken out of the recreation session, making play in fact a chore.

CONSEQUENCE CONDITIONS.   Recreation training may also be influenced by different types of reinforcement conditions. Although in some cases negative reinforcement (Whaley & Tough, 1970) and punishment (Koegel, Firestone, Kramme, & Dunlop, 1974) have been employed to decrease nonfunctional competing behaviors and to increase functional leisure-time skills, this discussion is limited to positive reinforcement conditions.

Positive Tangible Reinforcement. Edibles (Burney, Russell, & Shores, 1977; Kazdin & Erickson, 1975; Wehman et al., 1976), points (Knapczyk & Yoppi, 1975), and pennies (Wehman et al., 1976) have been used to develop ball rolling cooperative play, and ball throwing in developmentally disabled individuals. Although tangible reinforcers can be effective in shaping new leisure-time skills, they are recommended with the caution that it may be difficult to reduce the amount of reinforcer given, and that self-initiated spontaneous play does not occur under the control of artificial reinforcers such as tokens or edibles.

Social Reinforcement. Praise, attention, and approval from peers, parents, teachers, and other nonhandicapped trainers are potent motivators in developing and strengthening leisure-time activity (Strain, Cooke, Apolloni, 1976). Praise and physical affection were given in two studies which demonstrated the development of independent and social play in six institutionalized severely and profoundly retarded women (Wehman, 1977b). Praise and affection have also been used in numerous other studies (Morris & Dolker, 1974; Whitman et al. 1970; Williams et al. 1975). There are no controlled studies that assess the effects of peer reinforcement versus adult reinforcement and the specific learning characteristics of influential peers. Such studies are essential if we are to understand how to develop more natural reinforcement conditions in recreation sessions.

"Intrinsic" Reinforcement. Optimal reinforcement conditions in leisure time programming include those in which the toys, play materials, and games become naturally reinforcing. That is, appropriate leisure-time activity is best developed and maintained if play materials are intrinsically reinforcing. As mentioned in the section on assessment, few studies demonstrate the effective transfer of stimulus control from trainer cues to toys in the recreation environ-

ment (Hopper & Wambold, in press). The Premack Principle, or the contingent access to a high-preference leisure activity if a low reference activity is performed, may also be implemented in recreation sessions if students stereotype or play with the same material for long periods of time.

Of course, the above-mentioned techniques are best used in conjunction and should not be considered comprehensive. No pretense is made that these methods are novel or unique; in fact, they are simply behavior modification techniques that have been applied to other aspects of programming with the severely and profoundly handicapped. An attempt has been made here to describe techniques that can help severely handicapped students acquire free play skills. What is required is a specific assessment of which antecedent conditions and types of reinforcing conditions work best with students with different levels of play skills and learning characteristics.

TEACHING STRUCTURED RECREATION SKILLS

Task Analysis in Leisure-Time Programs

A growing body of research supports the training of the mentally retarded through use of task analysis (Gold, 1976; Williams, 1975). Task analysis is the breaking down of a skill into smaller behaviors. These behaviors are taught individually and then chained together as the child becomes more proficient at the skill. This allows for "part-learning" instead of "whole-learning"; learning in small chunks reduces the strain on the learner's memory and facilitates acquisition of new material (Blake, 1974).

There are numerous other advantages of the task analytic format of instruction (Knapczyk, 1975; McCormack, 1976). For example, determining the best point to begin instruction is facilitated by assessing the number of steps in the task sequence which the child demonstrated independently. Selecting the appropriate entry level skill for training is important because it minimizes the likelihood of teaching skills that are either too simplistic or too advanced (Edgar, Maser, Smith, & Haring, 1977). Task analysis is also a more systematic means of evaluating the effectiveness of a program because it provides an objective measure of how many steps were taught once instruction began.

Although task analysis is rapidly becoming accepted by special educators as a critical component of instructional programs, few leisure-time programs provide for the breakdown of recreational skills. This may be partly because much of play and leisure activity is free and spontaneous, and therefore not easily analyzed into smaller components. However, gross and fine-motor recreational skills, and also table games, are play behaviors that can be broken down into smaller responses. These skills can then be taught in an easy-to-hard sequence, with necessary modifications and adaptions made for students with different learning handicaps.

Developing a Task Analysis

Task analyses can be developed in a number of ways. Before attempting to analyze a behavior into smaller components, it is essential to review related program resource literature to evaluate whether task analyses have been previously developed (e.g., Williams, 1975). If no information is available, then consulting curriculum guides and child development texts for basic sequences in the relevant areas may be helpful. Many recreation activity texts for the handicapped are available (Amary, 1975) and can be used by those familiar with the task analysis format.

Brown and his associates (e.g., Brown, Bellamy, & Sontag, 1971) specified six steps to follow in generating a task analysis. This methodology is valid across skill areas and is recommended when developing recreational programs for the mentally retarded.

1. The teacher must specify terminal objectives in behavioristic terms; that is, she must convert the required criterion performance into observable responses.
2. The teacher must analyze the criterion responses and divide them into a series of less complex responses.
3. The teacher must arrange into a series the responses she decides are necessary to complete the terminal response.
4. The teacher must teach the student or verify his or her ability to perform each response in the series.
5. The teacher must teach the students to perform each response in the series in *serial* order.
6. In an attempt to delineate successes and failures, the teacher must record student performance during each training phase so that adjustments can be made during the teaching process. (Brown et al., p. 3)

Components of a Recreation Program

Effective recreation programs, which are instructional in nature, should include a behavioral objective (Mager, 1962), task analysis, the materials required, and the specific teaching procedures and environmental arrangement necessary to change behavior. Edginton and Hayes (1976) have done an excellent job of demonstrating how the three components of a performance objective—conditions, criterion, and behavioral description—can be applied to formulating objective recreation program goals.

Leisure programs that are more sophisticated in design may include a series of related task analyses that can be arranged into a skill sequence. One example of this would be a skill sequence of "old maid" in which task analyses for dealing cards, matching pictures, and shuffling were generated and then arranged into a logical order of presentation. Table 3–3 illustrates another example—ball-related activities that require increasing amounts of skill and proficiency.

Gross Motor Recreational Skill Development

Skills such as riding a tricycle, moving about on a scooter, jumping on a trampoline, and using playground equip-

---

Table 3–3. Ball-Related Skill Sequence

Task analysis A: ball rolling

Behavioral objective: The child will sit and roll the ball to the teacher in the first phase and to a peer in the second phase. The child will roll the ball 1 foot, then work his way up to 8 feet. The child must achieve 50% of the steps over a period of 3 consecutive days before moving on to another task. The task is completed when the child has achieved 90% of the steps.

Materials: Small ball, 8 inches in diameter; medium ball, 15 inches in diameter; large ball, 21 inches in diameter.

Steps:

1. Child sits on the floor.
2. Child holds the ball in front of his body with his fingers.
3. Child's body is facing the direction of the target person.
4. Child brings his arms back to the side of his body.
5. Ball is released by extending the fingers with palm of his hand facing the target person.
6. Child rolls ball by extending his arms.
7. Ball is rolled to target person 1 foot away.
8. Ball is rolled to target person 2 feet away.
9. Ball is rolled to target person 3 feet away.

10. Ball is rolled to target person 4 feet away.
11. Ball is rolled to target person 5 feet away.
12. Ball is rolled to target person 6 feet away.
13. Ball is rolled to target person 7 feet away.
14. Ball is rolled to target person 8 feet away.

Task analysis B: catching a ball

Objectives: When thrown a large rubber ball, the student will be able to catch the ball 95% of the time.

Materials: A large rubber ball.

Steps:

1. Student will bend his right arm at the elbow.
2. Student will bend his left arm at the elbow.
3. Student's forearms should be parallel.
4. Student's right palm should face outward.
5. Student's left palm should face outward.
6. Student should reach for the ball when it comes toward him, keeping his palms outward.
7. Student's right hand should move around the ball when the ball touches the student's hands.
8. Student's left hand should move around the ball.
9. Student will grasp the ball on impact.
10. Student's arms can move toward himself when the ball is caught.

---

ment, are important recreational behaviors for severely and profoundly handicapped students to acquire. These skills are not only fun and pleasurable, they also facilitate gross motor development and use of different muscles. Furthermore, they promote normal physical development and generally help the individual stay more healthy. A task analysis instructional strategy is an excellent means of teaching these skills. The following discussion involves the steps required in setting up a gross motor recreational program (Wehman & Marchant, 1977).

1. INFORMAL OBSERVATION.   An extended period of observation and consultation with occupational and physical therapists can help determine which students display the

necessary physical prerequisites to acquire selected gross motor skills. An effort should be made to select skills that require the use of a variety of muscles and gross motor movements, and which are thought to be within the student's capabilities.

As an illustration, consider a program that was initiated with severely and profoundly handicapped adults in a sheltered workshop (Wehman, Renzaglia, Schutz, & Karan, 1976). To break up parts of the 6-hour work day, it was decided to involve trainees in a structured exercise program during certain periods. Informal observation and assessment indicated that the trainees had poor muscle tone. The workers involved in this workshop program were rarely asked to perform any skills that required extensive physical activity. Therefore it was decided to teach basic physical fitness exercises such as push-ups and sit-ups.

2. GENERATING NECESSARY TASK ANALYSES.   Once specific skills within the gross motor domain are selected for instruction, task analyses must be developed. Frequently, task analyses that already exist do not have the detail required to teach the skill appropriately. In both the gross motor recreational skill program and the physical fitness program, it was necessary to consult texts on recreation and adaptive physical education (Daniels & Davies, 1975) for guidelines. From this information, we were then able to analyze the skill into more detailed components. Table 3–4 lists several gross motor recreational skill task analyses. Table 3–5 illustrates task analyses of three exercises which were taught in the earlier program.

3. TASK ANALYTIC ASSESSMENT.   The next step was to assess the trainees on each task analysis. This procedure can be done as follows. The teacher gives the general instruction: "Phil, show me how you ride the tricycle," or "Jean, show me how you do a sit-up." Each student can be assessed for

Table 3-4   Gross Motor Recreational Skills

Task analysis A: climbing ladder bars

Behavioral objective: The student will swing down playground ladder bars, by way of ladder rungs, 8 out of 10 times.

Steps:

1. Student approaches bars.
2. Student faces front end of bars.
3. With slight upward jump, student grasps rung of bars with right hand.
4. Student grasps second rung of bars with left hand.
5. Student extends right arm.
6. Student extends left arm.
7. Student alternates hand with each bar.
8. Student continues to alternate arm and hand until reaching the end of the bar.
9. When last hand reaches last bar, student releases bar.
10. Student lands on ground with feet in level position.

Task analysis B: swinging on a tire

Behavioral objective: The student will swing in a tire hanging from a tree by a rope 10 out of 10 times.

Steps:

1. Student approaches tire.
2. Student stands behind tire.
3. Student grasps rope with right hand.
4. Student grasps rope with left hand.
5. Left hand is placed slightly above right hand.
6. Student has both hands on rope (firm grip).
7. Student pulls self up.
8. Student sticks right leg into tire (still holding on to rope).
9. Student sticks left leg into tire.
10. Still holding on to rope, student pushes self forward.
11. Student swings back and forth.

Task analysis C: hula-hooping

Behavioral objective: The subject will hula-hoop 18 out of 20 times.

Steps:

1. Student approaches hoop.
2. Student stands in front of hoop.
3. With the hoop lying flat on the ground, student steps into center of hoop.

Table 3–4.   (Continued)

---

4. Student bends forward with hands extended to parallel edges of hoop.
5. Student grasps edge of hoop with right hand.
6. Student grasps other edge with left hand.
7. Student brings hoop to middle of body (waist).
8. Student twists body slightly to left.
9. Student grasps hoop firmly (with both hands).
10. Student plants feet in firm position, gives hoop a quick twirl, sending it around the body.
11. Student moves hips to left (right).
12. Student moves hips to back.
13. Student moves hips to right (left).
14. Student shifts hips forward.
15. Student moves body in a circular-like motion simultaneously with hoop.
16. Student continues moving body with hoop so that hoop goes around waist continuously.
17. After having met requirements, student brings hoop to a halt.
18. Student holds hoop with both hands (hoop still around waist).
19. Student lowers hoop back to flat position.
20. Hoop is lying around feet.
21. Student steps out of hoop, or
22. If hoop falls to ground (while hips are still in motion),
23. Lets hoop fall flatly on surface (around feet).
24. Student steps out of hoop.

---

the number of steps in each task analysis which he or she could perform independently, that is, with no physical or modeling assistance. From this assessment, the appropriate entry level skill for instruction can be determined.

Data may be collected at the middle or end of each assessment or instructional period. The student is asked to perform the given skill and receives a plus for each step completed independently and a minus for no response or for one in which assistance is required.

These figures can be expressed in percentages by dividing the total number of steps in the task analysis by the total number of steps performed independently, and then

Table 3-5.   Task Analyses of Exercises

Sit-ups:

1. Assume sitting position on mat.
2. Place hands behind head and lock fingers together.
3. Lie down on back.
4. Sit up with right elbow to left knee.
5. Lie down on back.
6. Sit up with left elbow to right knee.
7. Lie down on back.

Knee push-ups:

1. Get down on knees.
2. Put arms out in front on head.
3. Place legs up in air (balanced).
4. Put head down with legs up in air (through push-up position).
5. Bring head back up (to complete push-up).

Duck-walking:

1. Assume sitting position.
2. Bring knees up.
3. Put hands behind back with palms spread.
4. Push self up.
5. Push self up and take step.
6. Push self up and take three steps.
7. Push self up and walk lifting across room.
8. Push self up and duck-walk across room.

multiplying by 100. For a more detailed discussion of data collection methods, refer to an excellent article by Hanson and Bellamy (1977).

4. INSTRUCTIONAL PROCEDURES.   The instructional model which may be employed involves a basic sequence or continuum of teacher assistance. Initially, verbal instructions should be given to the student to perform the designated target step in the task analysis. If the student responds correctly, positive reinforcement is given immediately. If not, the target behavior is modeled or demonstrated by the

teacher. If this level of instruction still does not result in correct responding, manual guidance may be given.

Although this type of instruction has been successful in teaching severely handicapped students, a number of possible pitfalls can lead to breakdowns in learning or to programming problems. Several of these points are listed below as guidelines to those involved in implementing instructional procedures:

1. Do *all* staff understand how to implement the program?
2. Are *all* staff consistent in instruction?
3. Is an effective reinforcer being employed?
4. Is the reinforcer given immediately? Is praise *expressive?*
5. Does the student have an opportunity to consume an edible reinforcer before the next trial begins?
6. Do you have the student's attention before starting the next trial?
7. Is the student attending to the relevant part of the task or skill that you are teaching?
8. Are your language cues consistent and are they kept short? (In other words, be careful not to give irrelevant and distracting language cues.)
9. Are you giving instructions head-on to the student and facing her or him directly as you give instruction?
10. Have you broken down the skill into its smallest behavioral components?
11. Have you provided physical guidance too long and not begun to fade assistance appropriately?
12. Have you considered using extra cues to help the student learn, for example, colors to help attending to relevant part of the task?

13. Have you developed an easy-to-hard sequence of instruction? As an illustration, in teaching a student to use a balance beam, a wide board on the floor might be used initially and gradually faded to a more narrow beam. It could then be raised slightly off the floor.

5. MONITORING AND EVALUATION.   The daily collection of data allows for the careful monitoring of where progress is being made or where difficulties may be occurring. Ongoing evaluation of data facilitates the immediate modification of program procedures and subsequent changes, in teacher behaviors, if necessary.

Figure 3–3 charts the progress made by one student in learning three physical fitness exercises (Wehman, Renzaglia, Schultz, & Karan, 1976). A multiple baseline design was employed to evaluate the effectiveness of the teaching procedures across each exercise behavior (Kazdin, 1975).

Figure 3–4 tracks the acquisition of a ball-rolling skill in three students when small, large, and medium-sized balls were used. It should be evident that the change from small to large ball played an important part in the intervention. The ball-rolling task analysis reported in Table 3–3 was the sequence utilized in this program.

Developing a Repertoire of Table Game Skills

One leisure skill area that has received limited attention with severely handicapped persons is that of card games and table games. Nonetheless, this could be an excellent medium to promote socialization. Because of the interdependent nature of table games (Mithaug & Wolfe, 1976), students who do not usually engage in cooperative actions are more likely to do so in games that require two or more players. Furthermore, language skills (Bates, 1976) and

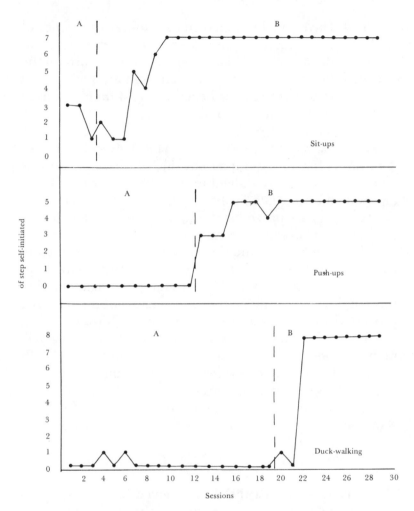

**Figure 3–3.   Self-initiated steps completed in three
exercises by Student 1.**

preacademic tasks (Thiagarajon, 1976) are most effectively
taught through learning selected table games.

Skepticism is the initial reaction to teaching table
games by many who work with severely and profoundly
handicapped students. This may well be an accurate sur-

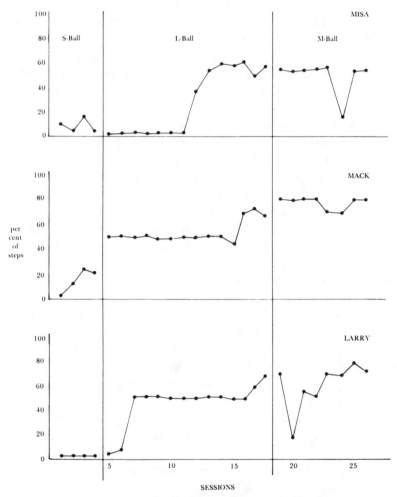

Figure 3–4. Percentage of steps acquired in a ball-rolling sequence by three students using a small ball, large ball, and medium-sized ball.

99

mise with many students, yet there are cases in which non-verbal students with seemingly limited academic potential have learned to play games such as candyland, hi-ho cher-ry-O, simple card games (Rankin, Bates, Baldwin, Kelly, & Hannah, 1975), tic-tac-toe, and checkers (Wehman, et al., 1976). The task analyses for tic-tac-toe and checkers can be found in Table 3–6, and Figure 3–5 depicts results of this table game training program.

So far the most exciting work in this area appears to be a master's thesis project performed by Paul Bates with a profoundly retarded institutionalized adolescent (Bates, 1976). The student was taught to play a modified table game in which he had to match pictures picked up from a deck of cards onto the game board. The purposes of the game were (1) to teach the student a cooperative leisure skill, (2) to facilitate the verbal imitation phase of the language program he was participating in, and (3) to teach him appropriate verbal labeling skills. Figure 3–6 represents the game board.

The basic teaching sequence was analyzed and divided into the following steps:

Step 1: Select a token moving piece. The student selects one moving piece from a box containing several of these items when given the general instruction, "Bob, it's time to play the word game."

Step 2: Place moving piece on "Go." The student places the moving piece in the circle designated "Go" on the game board.

Step 3: Pick one card. The student selects one card off the top of the deck of cards.

Step 4: Place card on table. The student turns the card face up on the table immediately in front of him.

Step 5: Verbally label the picture card. The student must make an intelligible approximation of the picture label.

Step 6: Move piece to picture card selected. The student

Table 3–6   Task Analyses of Table Games

Tic-tac-toe:

1. Remove all nine pegs from the board.
2. Choose either black or white pegs.
3. Place one peg in any hole in the peg board.
4. Watch partner place one peg in a hole in the peg board.
5. Place next piece next to own first piece so as to form a straight line across the board.
6. Block opponent's unfinished straight line by placing a peg in his attempted line.
7. Identify winner or stalemate.

Checkers:

1. Open box.
2. Unfold board.
3. Choose either black or red pieces.
4. Collect all 12 pieces.
5. Place in first three rows of red squares on board.
6. Move one man in forward direction.
7. Alternate turns.
8. Jump opponent's man in forward direction.
9. Remove opponent's checker from board.

Demonstrate ability to:

10. Move men so as not to get jumped.
11. Move men so as to jump opponent's checker.
12. Move men so as to jump opponent's checker and *not* get jumped in return.
13. Move men toward first row on opposite side of board.
14. "King" men by putting them on top of opponent's men when in his first row.
15. Move king in both forward and backward directions.

moves the piece clockwise to the first picture square that matches the picture card selected.

A backward chaining procedure was used to teach the different skills (Whaley & Malott, 1971). In this way the

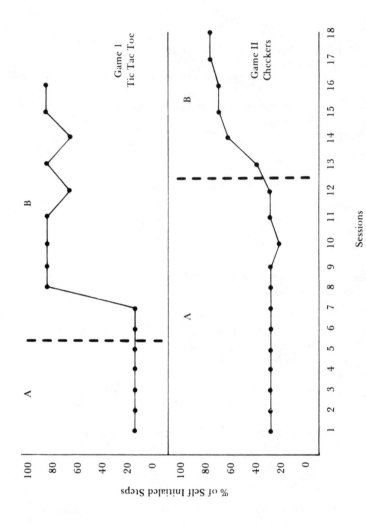

Figure 3–5. Self-initiated steps in two table games with Student 1.

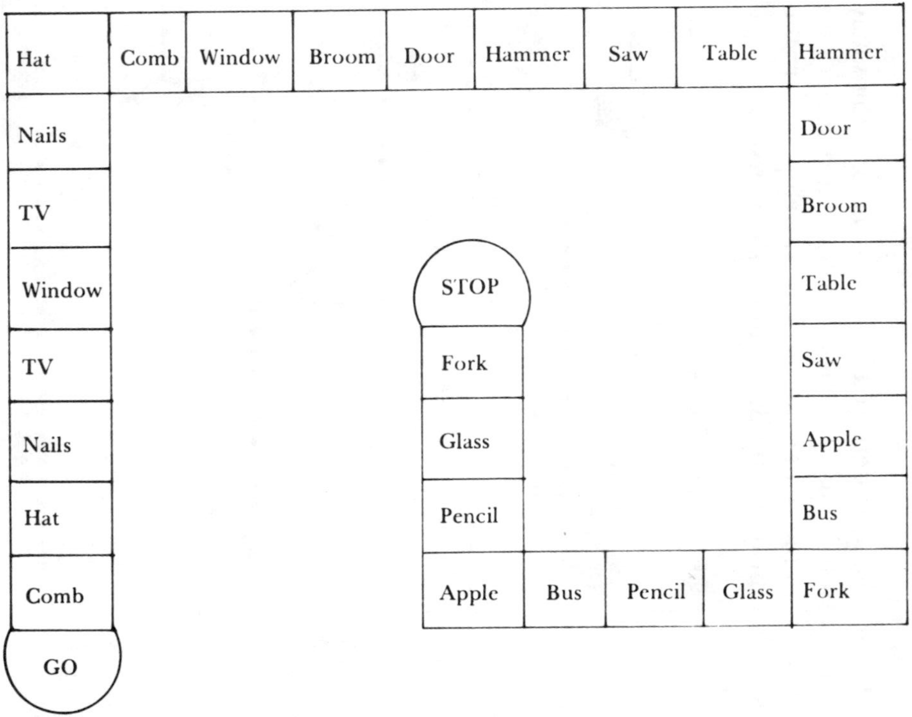

Figure 3–6. Picture of table game.

student was manually guided through most of the game and then received instruction at the end of the game. Figure 3–7 shows the results of the program, which were evaluated in a multiple baseline design across three different sets of words.

Those who are interested in table game programs may wish to consult Wehman (1977b), whose text includes a number of table game sequences developed for the severely handicapped by Bates and his coworkers.

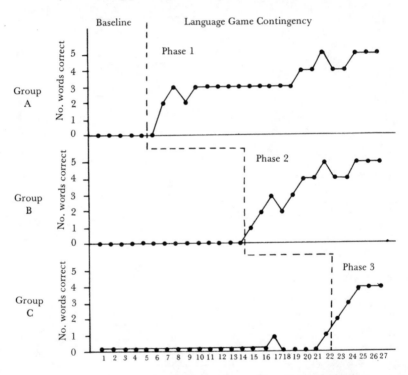

Figure 3–7.   The number of words verbally labeled correctly in Groups A, B, and C before and after implementation of the language game contingencies. Training words are substituted for the picture objects actually used in the game. The illustrated is scaled to one-third the size of the language game.

Conclusion

This chapter has tried to cover as many aspects as possible of play, leisure skills, and recreation with severely and profoundly handicapped persons. Clearly, many areas could have been discussed in far greater depth. Sports activities, community-based recreation programs, and arts and crafts activities are at least three major skill areas which were omitted because of lack of space but certainly not importance. The purpose of this chapter was to give some structure and organization to the area of recreation programming. There is little doubt that the overlap between leisure skills and sensory motor awareness, fine and gross motor skill development, and language development is indeed substantial.

References

Amary, I. *Creative recreation for the mentally retarded.* Springfield, Illinois: Charles C. Thomas, 1975.

Baer, D., Peterson, R. F., & Sherman, J. The development of imitation by reinforcing behavioral similarity to a model. *Journal of the Experimental Analysis of Behavior,* 1967, *10,* 405–416.

Bandura, A. *Principles of behavior modification.* New York: Holt, Rinehart and Winston, 1969.

Barnes, K. Preschool play norms: A replication. *Developmental Psychology,* 1971, *5,* 99–103.

Bates, P. Language instruction with a profoundly retarded adolescent: The use of a table game in the acquisition, generalization, and maintenance of verbal labeling skills. Unpublished master's thesis, Department of Studies in Behavioral Disabilities, University of Wisconsin, Madison, Wisconsin, 1976.

Blake, K. A. *Teaching the retarded.* Englewood Cliffs, N.J.: Prentice-Hall, 1974.

Brown, L., Bellamy, G. T., & Sontag, E. *The development and implementation of a public school prevocational training program for trainable retarded and severely emotionally disturbed children.* Madison, Wisconsin, Madison Public Schools, 1971.

Burney, J., Russell, B., & Shores, R. Developing social responses in two profoundly retarded children. *AAESPH Review,* 1977, *2(2),* 53–64.

Cataldo, M., & Risley, T. Infant day care. In Ulrich, R., Stachnik, T., & Mosley, R. (Eds.), *Control of Human Behavior* (Vol. III). Glenview, Illinois: Scott, Foresman and Company, 1974.

Cooke, T., & Apolloni, T. Developing positive social-emotional behaviors: A study of training and generalization. *Journal of Applied Behavior Analysis,* 1976, *9,* 65–78.

Daniels, A., & Davies, G. *Adapted physical education.* New York: Harper & Row, 1975.

Edgar, E., Maser, J., Smith, D., & Haring, N. G. Developing an instructional sequence for teaching a self-help skill. *Education and Training of the Mentally Retarded,* 1977, *12(1),* 42–51.

Edginton, C., & Hayes, G. Using performance objectives in the delivery of therapeutic recreation services. *Journal of Leisureability,* 1976, *3(4),* 20–26.

Ellis, M. J. *Why people play.* Englewood Cliffs, New Jersey: Prentice-Hall, Inc., 1973.

Favell, J., & Cannon, P. An evaluation of entertainment materials for severely retarded persons. *American Journal of Mental Deficiency,* 1977, *81,* 357–362.

Gardner, W. I. *Behavior modification in mental retardation.* Chicago: Aldine-Atherton, 1971.

Gardner, W. I. *Children with learning and behavior problems.* Boston: Allyn & Bacon, 1974.

Gesell, A. *The first five years of life.* New York: Harper, 1940.

Gibson, F., Lawrence, P., & Nelson, R. Comparison of three training precedures for teaching social responses to developmentally disabled adults. *American Journal of Mental Deficiency,* 1977, *81,* 379–387.

Gilhool, T. Changing public policies in the individualization of instruction: Roots and forces. *Education and Training of the Mentally Retarded,* 1976, *11,* 180–188.

Goetz, E., & Baer, D. Social control of form diversity and the emergence of new forms in children's block building. *Journal of Applied Behavior Analysis,* 1973, *6,* 209–217.

Gold, M. W. Task analysis of a complex assembly task by the retarded blind. *Exceptional Children,* 1976, *43(2),* 78–87.

Hamre-Nietupski, S., & Williams, W. W. Teaching selected sex education and social skills to severely handicapped students. In L. Brown, N. Certo, K. Belmore, & T. Crowner (Eds.), *Madison's alternative to zero exclusion: Papers and programs related to public school services for second-*

ary age severely handicapped students (Vol. VI, Part I). Madison, Wisconsin: Madison Public Schools, 1976.

Hanson, M., & Bellamy, G. T. Continuous measurement of progress in infant intervention programs. *Education and Training of the Mentally Retarded,* 1977, *12(1),* 52–58.

Hopper, C., & Wambold, C. An applied approach to improving the independent play behavior of severely mentally retarded children. *Education and Training of the Mentally Retarded,* in press.

Horner, R. D., & Keilitz, I. Training mentally retarded adolescents to brush their teeth. *Journal of Applied Behavior Analysis,* 1975, *8,* 301–310.

Hunter, J., & Bellamy, G. T. Cable harness construction for severely retarded adults: A demonstration of training technique, *AAESPH Review,* 1976, *1(7),* 2–13.

Hurlock, E. *Child development* (5th ed.). New York: McGraw-Hill, 1972.

Kazdin, A. E. *Behavior modification in applied settings.* Homewood, Illinois: Dorsey Press, 1975.

Kazdin, A. E., & Erickson, B. Developing responsiveness to instructions in severely and profoundly retarded residents. *Journal of Behavior Therapy and Experimental Psychiatry,* 1975, *6,* 17–21.

Kazdin, A. E., Silverman, N., & Sittler, J. The use of prompts to enhance vicarious effects of nonverbal approval. *Journal of Applied Behavior Analysis,* 1975, *8,* 279–286.

Knapczyk, D. Task analytic assessment of severe learning problems. *Education and Training of the Mentally Retarded,* 1975, *10(3),* 74–77.

Knapczyk, D., & Peterson, N. Social play interaction of retarded children in an integrated classroom environment. Unpublished manuscript, Developmental Training Center, University of Indiana, Bloomington, Indiana, 1975.

Knapczyk, D., & Yoppi, J. Development of cooperative and competitive play responses in developmentally disabled children. *American Journal of Mental Deficiency,* 1975, *80,* 245–255.

Knowles, C., Vogel, P., & Wessel, J. Project I CAN: Individualized curriculum designed for mentally retarded children and youth. *Education and Training of the Mentally retarded,* 1975, *10,* 155–160.

Koegel, R., Firestone, P., Kramme, K. R., Dunlop, G. Increasing, spontaneous play by suppressing self-stimulation in autistic children. *Journal of Applied Behavior Analysis,* 1974, *1,* 521–528.

Mager, R. F. *Preparing instructional objectives.* Palo Alto, California: Fearon, 1962.

McCall, R. Exploratory manipulation and play in the human infant.

Monograph of the Society for Research in Child Development. Chicago: University of Chicago Press, 1974.

McCormack, J. Using a task analysis format to develop instructional sequences. *Education and Training of the Mentally Retarded,* 1976, *11(4),* 318–323

Mithaug, D., & Wolfe, M. S. Employing task arrangements and verbal contingencies to promote verbalizations between retarded children. *Journal of Applied Behavior Analysis,* 1976, *9(3),* 301–314.

Morris, R., & Dolker, M. Developing cooperative play in socially withdrawn retarded children. *Mental Retardation,* 1974, *12,* 24–27.

Nelson, R., Gibson, F., & Cutting, D. Videotaped modeling: The development of three appropriate social responses in a mildly retarded child. *Mental Retardation,* 1973, *11(3),* 24–27.

Paloutzian, R. F., Hasazi, J., Streifel, J., & Edgar, C. Promotion of positive social interaction in severely retarded young children. *American Journal of Mental Deficiency,* 1971, *75,* 519–524.

Parten, M. B. Social play among preschool children. *Journal of Abnormal Psychology,* 1932, *28,* 136–147.

Piaget, J. *Play, dreams and imitation in childhood.* New York: W. W. Norton, 1951.

Quilitch, H. R., & Risley, T. The effects of play materials on social play. *Journal of Applied Behavior Analysis,* 1973, *6,* 573–578.

Rankin, C., Bates, P., Baldwin, D., Kelly, T., & Hannah, S. Table games for institutionalized severely retarded adolescents. Unpublished manuscript, Lincoln Developmental Center, Lincoln, Illinois, 1975.

Redd, W. H. Effects of mixed reinforcement on adults' control of children's behavior. *Journal of Applied Behavior Analysis,* 1969, *2,* 249–254.

Snyder, L., Apolloni, T., & Cooke, T. Integrated settings at the early childhood level: The role of nonretarded peers. *Exceptional Children,* 1977, *43(5),* 262–269.

Strain, P., Cooke, T., & Apolloni, T. *Teaching exceptional children: Assessment and modification of social behavior,* New York: Academic Press, 1976.

Thiagarajan, S. Designing instructional games for handicapped learners. *Focus on Exceptional Children,* 1976, *7.*

Tilton, J., & Ottinger, D. Comparison of toy play behavior of autistic, retarded, and normal children. *Psychological Reports,* 1964, *15,* 967–975.

Twardosz, S., Cataldo, M., & Risley, T. An open environment design for infant and toddler day care. *Journal of Applied Behavior Analysis,* 1974, *7,* 529–546.

Wehman, P. Establishing play behaviors in mentally retarded youth. *Rehabilitation Literature,* 1975, *36,* 238–246.

Wehman, P. Selection of play materials for the severely handicapped: A continued dilemma. *Education and Training of the Mentally Retarded,* 1976. *11(1),* 46–51. (a)

Wehman, P. Imitation as a facilitator of treatment for the mentally retarded. *Rehabilitation Literature,* 1976, *37(2),* 41–48. (b)

Wehman, P. *Helping the mentally retarded acquire play skills: A behavioral approach.* Springfield, Illinois: Charles C. Thomas, 1977. (a)

Wehman, P. Research on leisure time and the severely developmentally disabled. *Rehabilitation Literature,* 1977, *38(4),* 98–105. (b)

Wehman, P. Effects of different environmental conditions on leisure time activity of the severely and profoundly handicapped. *Journal of Special Education,* 1978, *12(2).*

Wehman, P., Karan, O., & Rettie, C. Developing independent play in three severely retarded women. *Psychological Reports,* 1976, *39,* 995–998.

Wehman, P., Renzaglia, A., Schutz, R., & Karan, O. Training leisure time skills in severely and profoundly handicapped adolescents: Three recreation programs. In O. Karan, P. Wehman, A. Renzaglia, & R. Schutz (Eds.) *Habilitation practices with the severely developmentally disabled.* Madison, Wisconsin: University of Wisconsin Rehabilitation Research and Training Center, 1976.

Wehman, P., & Marchant, J. Developing gross motor recreational skills in severely and profoundly handicapped children. Paper presented at the Virginia State Council on Exceptional Children Convention, Roanoke, Virginia, March, 1977.

Wehman, P., & Marchant, J. Improving free play skills of severely and profoundly retarded adolescents. *American Journal of Occupational Therapy,* 1978, *32(2),* 100–104.

Whaley, D., & Malott, R. *Elementary principles of behavior.* New York: Appleton-Century-Crofts, 1971.

Whaley, D., & Tough, J. Treatment of a self-injuring mongoloid with shock-induced suppression and avoidance. Michigan Department of Mental Health, 1968, *4,* 18–28.

White, O., & Liberty, K. Behavioral assessment and precise educational measurement. In N. Haring & R. Schiefelbusch (Eds.), *Teaching special children,* New York: McGraw-Hill, 1976.

Whitman, T. L., Mercurio, J. R., & Caponigri, V. Development of social responses in two severely retarded children. *Journal of Applied Behavior Analysis,* 1970, *3,* 133–138.

Williams, W. W. Procedures of task analysis as related to developing instructional programs for the severely handicapped. In L. Brown, T. Crowner, W. Williams, & R. York (Eds.), *Madison's alternative to zero exclusion: A book of readings.* Madison, Wisconsin: Madison Public Schools, 1975.

Williams, W. W., Pumpian, I., McDaniel, J., Hamre-Nietupski, S., & Wheeler, J. Social interaction. In L. Brown, T. Crowner, W. Williams, & R. York (Eds.) *Madison's alternative to zero exclusion: A book of readings.* Madison, Wisconsin: Madison Public Schools, 1975.

Zine, B., Ferolo, M., Hass, S., & Hass, W. Free play responses of profoundly retarded children to pre-recorded broadcast children's songs. *Journal of Developmental Disabilities,* 1975, *1,* 19–22.

Chapter 4

VOCATIONAL EDUCATION

There is a growing emphasis on vocational training programs for severely handicapped adolescents and adults. State and federal agencies are allocating large sums of money for vocational rehabilitation programs to serve the severely handicapped. This is, to a large extent, a result of recent legislation that mandates increased vocational rehabilitation of the severely handicapped (Rehabilitation Act of 1973, P.L. 93–112). The push to rehabilitate many individuals by or through necessity once thought beyond the scope of most rehabilitation agencies has perforce raised the question of what to expect from these clients. It is difficult to evaluate programs and establish accountability without knowing what severely handicapped persons can do and what potential they have for habilitation.

It is a common belief of professionals in many rehabilitation settings that the severely handicapped can perform only the simplest of tasks. In recent years, however, significant progress has been made in the vocational training of severely and profoundly handicapped workers (e.g., Bellamy, 1976; Karan, Wehman, Renzaglia, & Schutz, 1976). This chapter reviews some of these recent advances in the vocational training the severely handicapped.

WHAT IS THE POTENTIAL OF SEVERELY HANDICAPPED WORKERS?

An increasing amount of research evidence suggests that severely and profoundly handicapped individuals can be effective workers on complex manual tasks (Gold, 1973a; 1976; Hunter & Bellamy, 1976). Several researchers have taught severely handicapped workers such complex tasks as putting together drill machines (Crosson, 1969) and bicycle brakes (Gold & Barclay, 1973). In the Crosson (1969) study, a 16-step task analysis was utilized to teach adolescents how to put a drill machine together. Brown and his associates have also used task analysis in studying the effects that different reinforcement contingencies have on production rates with moderately and severely handicapped adolescents (Brown, Bellamy, Perlmutter, Sackowitz, & Sontag, 1972; Brown, Perlmutter, Van Deventer, Jones, & Sontag, 1972).

Gold has demonstrated the effectiveness of moderately to severely handicapped trainees in complex work tasks (1973a). Through errorless learning, or easy-to-hard discriminations, moderately to severely handicapped adults were trained to put together a 15-piece bicycle brake (Gold, 1972). At a later point, subjects demonstrated successful transfer of training by putting together a 24-piece bicycle brake. A one year follow-up study indicated significant retention by the workers.

The same research program also showed that moderately to severely handicapped workers were able to discriminate between different bolt lengths as fine as one-eighth of an inch (Gold & Barclay, 1973). First workers were taught to distinguish gross differences of bolt length (i.e., ½ inch versus 3 inches long), and gradually the amount of discrimination required was increased. Gold (1973b) reports the success of 20 moderately to severely handicapped workers in putting together a 14-piece coaster brake. An important finding of this study was a nonsignificant statistical relationship between IQ and production rates of workers participating in the program. This result directly conflicts with earlier reports which supported the notion that higher IQs lead to greater production rates in handicapped workers (Tobias & Gorelick, 1963).

In another line of research, also in the area of training workers in the acquisition of complex manual skills, Bellamy and his associates (Bellamy, Peterson, & Close, 1975; Hunter & Bellamy, 1976; Irvin, 1976) conducted a series of studies using training techniques similar to Gold's, but with different tasks. Cable harness and cam switch actuator assembly were among the tasks utilized. The general training strategy was to teach either in small steps or in sequential "chunks" of the task analysis.

The work of Bellamy and associates provides an outstanding extension of the earlier studies of Gold. Color coding and easy-to-hard sequencing have been utilized as instructional techniques to facilitate the acquisition of complex skills. For example, in learning to place a certain nut with a particular size bolt, the trainer might attach a red mark to the bolt. The addition of the color cue and the easy-to-hard sequencing described above have proved to be highly effective (e.g., Irvin & Bellamy, 1977).

From this brief discussion of recent vocational research, it should be apparent that severely handicapped workers do have the work potential necessary to acquire complex as well as simple manual work skills. What is required are powerful training procedures that employ the principles of discrimination learning and operant conditioning.

BEHAVIORAL TRAINING STRATEGIES

The previous section described the potential of severely handicapped workers with an emphasis on the learning of new skills. Once specific work skills are acquired, however, the skill must be performed at a high enough rate to meet competitive employment standards. Since there are a number of training techniques that can increase production rates, as well as facilitate acquisition, it is necessary to analyze the type of problem that a worker is exhibiting. From this analysis, a behavioral strategy can be selected to remedy the problem (Wehman, Renzaglia, & Schutz, 1977).

Presenting Problems

ACQUISITION PROBLEM—DISCRIMINATION DEFICITS. A typical problem with many severely handicapped workers is a failure to attend to the salient cues (size, color, form) of a task. Relevant variables are ignored, and instead the person may try to assemble or sort materials without watching what he does, or to attend to the wrong cue in the task. As Gold (1973a) notes, this is the main obstacle for the mentally retarded in acquiring complex manual skills. Gold (1972) also found that the retarded can master a difficult job as quickly as nonretarded peers when they attend to relevant dimensions.

Acquisition can also be impeded by a worker's failure to attend to verbal cues of the supervisor. A common characteristic of severely handicapped adults is noncompliance behavior and inability or unwillingness to follow simple instructions. Even though a worker may attend to the learning task, failure to follow instructions can interfere with acquisition rates. This is particularly true if job requirements or materials vary slightly from day to day.

ACQUISITION PROBLEM—SENSORY MOTOR DEFICITS. Many severely handicapped persons involved in vocational programming also display sensory-motor deficits. Cerebral palsy, loss of limbs, and spasticity or athetosis call for prostheses or specially arranged environmental supports.

Certain workers may be visually handicapped or suffer a hearing loss; either may prohibit the use of standard training procedures. The rare combination of both aural and visual handicaps in retarded workers is perhaps the most difficult disability to overcome in acquiring complex work skills. Yet some workers have found that such disabilities need not impede learning progress on difficult tasks such as bicycle brake assembly (Gold, 1976).

LOW PRODUCTION—SLOW MOTOR BEHAVIOR. Once a vocational task is mastered, a high rate of performance becomes important. This is a serious problem with many severely and profoundly retarded workers, particularly those with a long history of institutionalization. Slow motor behavior is one characteristic of severely handicapped workers who have not been required to meet a work criterion for success. Workers may be persistent and stay on the task, but actual motor movements are lethargic and far too slow to allow competitive employment. Often such workers are unresponsive to many of the commonly used workshop incentives such as praise or money.

Without objectively established work criteria, it is difficult for workshop supervisors to determine which workers are performing competitively. Workers who stay on a task and do not disrupt workshop routine are viewed as performing adequately. This is based on a popular vocational training model of "work activity or keep-busy" rather than on a developmental model aimed at expanding the worker's repertoire of skills.

LOW PRODUCTION—INTERFERING BEHAVIORS.   An equally difficult problem in accelerating the production rates of the severely and profoundly handicapped is an interfering or competing behavior. High levels of distractability and hyperactivity, out-of-seat behavior, excessive looking around, bizarre noises, and playing with the task are competing behaviors that preclude the development of appropriate vocational skills.

Similarly, the work performance of severely handicapped workers may be highly susceptible to changes in the work environment. Fairly commonplace alterations in the work setting or routine, such as furniture rearrangement, can upset the behavior of workers and thus make programming continuity extremely difficult. Many others may display criterion-level work rates but only for short times. Interfering or competing behaviors interrupt the work level required for successful community placement.

Specific Training Techniques for Alleviating Work Problems

To meet these various workshop problems with severely and profoundly handicapped workers, a logically arranged sequence of training and behavior management procedures is required. This section lists several techniques and guidelines for alleviating these problems. Through systematic arrangement of these procedures into hierarchical order, workshop staff may draw on the techniques that are most effective, least time consuming, and most economical. The order of sequencing is also affected by traditional methods of alleviating problems within the world of competitive employment. The less severe or more typical training and management procedures are listed as the most desirable.

For example, a verbal reprimand (Schutz, Wehman, Renzaglia, & Karan, in press) would be preferred to the use of restraint if both procedures were equally effective in alleviating the problem. However, it may be necessary for a trainer to use his or her own discretion with each individual worker in determining which procedure is the most appropriate. If a trainer has had previous experience with a particular worker and has found that a verbal reprimand *increases* inappropriate behaviors (e.g., Madsen, Becker, Thomas, Koser, & Plager, 1970), it would be more beneficial to begin with the next technique in the hierarchy to ensure success.

Table 4–1 summarizes the proposed hierarchy of training and behavior management procedures for ameliorating workshop problems. These are hierarchically arranged for each problem area.

ACQUISITION PROBLEM—DISCRIMINATION DEFICITS.   The most frequently used training method in competitive employment is verbal instruction. Many times a new task will be acquired with only a verbal explanation. This should logically be the initial method used to teach a new task. If unsuccessful, a trainer must try alternate methods.

Illustrations of this approach include verbal instructions paired with modeling of the correct movements (Bellamy, Peterson, & Close, 1975; Clarke & Hermelin, 1956), priming the response, and physical guidance (Williams, 1967). Breaking a task down into small, measurable components (task analysis) is also an effective technique for aiding acquisition (Crosson, 1969; Gold, 1972), as is the method of presenting learning material in an easy-to-hard sequence (Gold & Barclay, 1973; Irvin, 1976). With workers who fail to attend to relevant cues or task dimensions,

Table 4-1. A Logically Arranged Hierarchy of Procedures for Alleviating Work Problems

Learning or acquisition problems—discrimination deficits

1. Verbal instructions
2. Model and verbal
3. Verbal and physical guidance
4. Break task down into simpler steps (easy-to-hard sequence) and repeat steps 1–3
5. Cue redundancy or stimulus fading depending on task
6. Steps 1–5 are always accompanied by reinforcement for correct responding

Learning or acquisition problems due to sensory-motor deficits (assess handicap to be sure there is a physical problem)

A. Poor motor coordination
   1. Verbal instructions
   2. Model and verbal
   3. Physical and verbal
   4. Break task down into simpler steps (easy-to-hard sequence) and repeat steps 1–3
   5. Prosthetic device or physical arrangement of materials
   6. Cue redundancy or stimulus fading
   7. Same as above step 6

B. Visually handicapped
   1. Verbal instructions (detailed)
   2. Physical guidance and verbal instructions
   3. Tactile cue redundancy and repeat steps 1 and 2

C. Acoustically handicapped
   1. Gestural instructions
   2. Physical guidance
   3. Break task down into simpler steps (easy-to-hard sequence) and repeat steps 1 and 2
   4. Cue redundancy or stimulus fading depending on task

D. Deaf/blind
   1. Physical guidance
   2. Tactile cue redundancy

Table 4-1. (Continued)

Low production—slow motor behavior

1. Verbal prompt (e.g., "work faster")
2. Verbal plus model
3. Physical prompt (paired with verbal)
4. Reinforcer proximity
   a. Pennies on hand
   b. Back-up also on hand
5. Increase frequency of giving pennies
6. Increase amount of pennies and/or back-ups
7. Increase frequency of redemption of pennies
8. Verbal reprimand plus no reinforcement
9. Response cost
10. Isolation/avoidance
11. Positive practice
12. Presentation of aversive stimuli

Low production—interfering or excessive behavior

Representative classes include
   a. Nonfunctional competing behavior
   b. Bizarre noises
   c. Out-of-seat behavior
   d. Aggression against objects
   e. Aggression against people
1. Verbal reprimand and prompt
2. Verbal reprimand and physical prompt
3. Reinforcement proximity (pennies then back-up)
4. Increase frequency of receiving reinforcement (pennies)
5. Increase amount of pennies and/or back-up
6. Increase frequency of redemption
7. Response cost
8. Time-out
9. Restraint
10. Overcorrection/positive practice
11. Isolation/avoidance
12. Presentation of aversive stimuli

the use of cue redundancy, e.g. color-coded parts, facilitates acquisition (Gold, 1974).

ACQUISITION PROBLEM—SENSORY-MOTOR DEFICITS.   In meeting the needs of workers with sensory-motor deficits, the worker's physical capacity must be the first consideration. When poor motor coordination is due to cerebral palsy or loss of limb, the first four suggested strategies in the hierarchy do not differ from those used with workers whose acquisition problems are due to discrimination deficits. However, if the worker's physical limitations are extensive, the arrangement of materials or the use of prosthetic devices such as specially designed jigs may be a crucial factor in the acquisition of vocational skills (Hollis, 1967). It may be necessary for a trainer to modify the task so that workers are able to complete a task with the least effort and most speed.

LOW PRODUCTION—SLOW MOTOR BEHAVIOR.   As workers become more proficient at performing a task, the goal becomes increasing the rate of production to competitive employment standards. The severely developmentally disabled must produce at a competitive level to find and maintain community workshop employment. A verbal prompt to work faster appears to be the least time consuming and most efficient technique, if the worker heeds the instruction (Bellamy et al., 1975). Peer modeling (Brown & Pearce, 1970; Kliebahn, 1967) and trainer modeling have also helped increase production rate.

The manipulation of reinforcing events offers another extensive array of possible techniques. Reinforcer proximity, increasing the frequency of the amount of reinforcement, and increasing the number of redemptions of token reinforcers in a work period all seem to be logical techniques for increasing production rates (e.g., Schroeder, 1972). Furthermore, my experience indicates that mixed schedules of reinforcement such as continuous social reinforcement for each unit completed, and penny or token reinforcement for every ten units completed, can be extremely effective in altering production rates with the severely handicapped (Wehman, Renzaglia, Schutz, & Karan, 1976). Figure 4–1 indicates the effectiveness of a reinforcement program on the production of a profoundly retarded worker.

However, if the problem of low production rates persists, it may be necessary to provide aversive consequences. Once a trainer has established a level of expectancy or a minimum production rate, the use of aversive consequences may be appropriate. Implementing a verbal reprimand procedure and no reinforcement (Schutz et al., in press) or a response cost procedure for low production may be effective if used in conjunction with positive consequences for acceptable work rates. With an established minimum criterion for performance, an isolation-avoidance procedure may also be used successfully (Zimmerman, Overpeck, Eisenberg, & Garlick, (1969). An isolation-avoidance procedure entails removing the worker from the work area if a designated work criterion is not met.

Because low production is often a result of slow motor behavior, which is characteristic of the severely and profoundly handicapped, a positive practice overcorrection with the intent of teaching fast motor behavior is a feasible alternative (e.g., Rusch & Close, 1976). This requires guiding the worker through a task a number of times in succession at a fast rate, and thereby teaching a worker to move with speed. If this procedure is implemented, a trainer must take care to make the physical guidance sufficiently unpleasant so that it is not socially reinforcing to a worker. This technique was recently tried with a profoundly retarded adolescent, and it increased production rates by 200 percent (Wehman, Schutz, Renzaglia, & Karan, 1977).

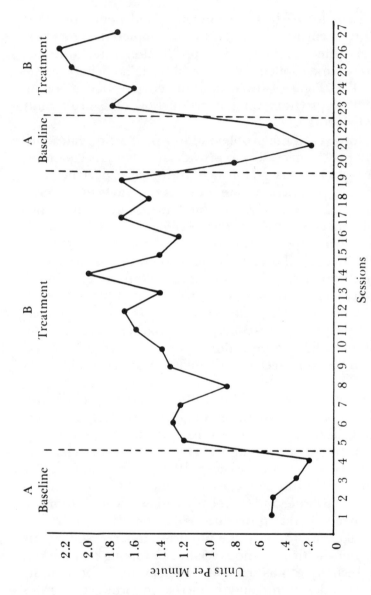

Figure 4-1. The production rate of a profoundly retarded worker under reinforcement (treatment) conditions.

LOW PRODUCTION—INTERFERING BEHAVIORS   A low production rate as a result of nonfunctional competing behaviors poses a somewhat different problem. A trainer must not only increase a worker's work rate but also decrease or preferably eliminate the amount of time a worker spends in the interfering behaviors. Manipulating different parameters of reinforcement may also be effective in alleviating this problem. Unfortunately, there is little or no published research that describes efforts to overcome excessive distractability by developmentally disabled workers in vocational settings.

To decrease many interfering behaviors, it may be necessary to implement aversive consequences. The use of response cost (Kazdin, 1973b), time-out (MacDonough & Forehand, 1973), restraint, and positive practice overcorrection (Azrin, Gottlieb, Hughart, Wesolowski, & Rahn, 1975; Wehman et al, 1977)—as immediate consequences of engaging in interfering behaviors—may successfully decrease stereotypic behavior, aggression, out-of-seat behavior, and bizarre noises. These procedures have been effective with several handicapped populations in different settings, and they should be seriously considered in workshops for the severely developmentally disabled.

COMPONENTS OF AN EFFECTIVE VOCATIONAL TRAINING PROGRAM FOR THE SEVERELY HANDICAPPED

In sum, a review of the existing vocational skill research with severely handicapped workers indicates that there are several integral components in successful training programs. These elements are briefly outlined and discussed as an aid to those faced with the vocational education of the severely and profoundly handicapped.

1. Task analysis is instrumental in making the job easier for the worker, thus increasing the probability of suc-

cess. Breaking a social skill or work task into smaller, logically sequenced increments allows the severely retarded individual to absorb the information more easily. The small increments of behavior are gradually chained together through reinforcement and thus develop the whole skill. It would appear that in vocational programming with low-functioning retarded persons, work tasks should be task analyzed by the teachers before training sessions begin. Eventually, a program notebook of task analyses can be completed and prescribed for each worker. Examples of two vocational related task analyses can be found in Tables 4–2 and 4–3.

2. A high degree of structure in the vocational setting and consistency in the approach of trainers in the initial stages are necessary for optimal performance. Instructions must be consistent and there should be little variation in the methods of presentation and criterion for reinforcement. Initially, the physical environment should be a setting with few distractions.

Reinforcers must be individualized for each worker, and it must be clear that they are instrumental in increasing behavior. Often it is difficult to discern what reinforcers will influence the behavior of severely handicapped persons. The teacher must test out different reinforcers and evaluate the effect of each on work performance. Presenting a variety of functional reinforcers initially, on a continuous schedule of reinforcement, and gradually on a more intermittent schedule will result in acquisition of the desired vocational behavior.

3. Vocational programs that utilize carefully gathered data of worker's performance are most effective in helping to make program modifications and decisions. The severely handicapped make behavioral gains slowly, and the evaluation of program methods is usually subjective and not

Table 4-2.   Stuffing Envelopes

Objective: Given a 9½ × 4 inch envelope, the student will insert the pre-folded 11 × 8½ inch paper into the envelope four out of five times within 3 days.

Steps:

1. Student picks up envelope.
2. Student turns envelope so that flap opening is faced toward the student.
3. Student places envelope in above position on flat surface.
4. Student places folded paper adjacent to envelope with top flap free to open.
5. Student places right hand on right side of folded paper.
6. Student maintains thumb on front of paper, sliding four fingers to back of folded paper.
7. Student lifts folded paper with right hand in above position to a position over the envelope.
8. Student places left hand on envelope flap.
9. Student pushes envelope flap back.
10. Student lifts hand from flap.
11. Student places left hand on top left corner of envelope.
12. Student slips four fingers into envelope, maintaining thumb on front of envelope.
13. Student pulls envelope up.
14. Student brings folded paper down over the envelope with right hand.
15. Student inserts left-hand bottom corner of folded paper into opened left side of envelope with right hand.
16. Student pushes folded paper halfway down with right hand.
17. Student places right hand on center of folded paper.
18. Student pushes folded paper all the way down into envelope.

carefully documented. There are several steps to making a databased approach to programming work to your advantage:

    a.   gain an accurate pretreatment index of the degree (frequency) of behavior.

    b.   the behavior must be defined clearly, and it must be discrete and observable.

Table 4–3. Washing Windows

Objective: Given a pail, sink, detergent, sponge, and newspaper, the student will wash a 2 × 2 inch window in 15 minutes, 95 percent of the time.

Steps:

1. Student takes pail in hand.
2. Student takes pail to sink.
3. Student places pail under water spigot.
4. Student turns hot water on.
5. Student turns cold water on.
6. Student allows pail to get half full of water.
7. Student turns hot water off.
8. Student turns cold water off.
9. Student takes pail from sink.
10. Student measures three-quarters of a cup of detergent.
11. Student pours detergent into pail of water.
12. Student puts sponge into water.
13. Student takes pail and approaches the window.
14. Student takes newspaper over to window.
15. Student puts newspaper beside pail.
16. Student takes sponge out of water.
17. Student squeezes sponge a little to get dripping water.
18. Student places sponge on top of left-hand corner of window.

c. Gradual improvements can be charted and graphed, and thus provide positive feedback to staff and parents.

d. Length of treatment can be identified precisely, as can the effects of treatment on behavior.

e. An objective index of accountability is gained with parents and administrators.

4. Methods that facilitate the transfer of training and response maintenance must be planned and developed within the overall program. It cannot be expected to occur spontaneously. As mentioned earlier, severely retarded in-

19. Student pulls sponge down against left fourth of window.
20. Student brings sponge up to the top again.
21. Student places sponge on the second fourth of the window.
22. Student pulls sponge down to the bottom of the window.
23. Student brings sponge up to the top again.
24. Student places sponge on the third fourth of the window.
25. Student pulls sponge down to the bottom again.
26. Student places sponge on the top right-hand corner of window.
27. Student pulls sponge down to the bottom.
28. Student puts sponge back into pail.
29. Student picks up newspaper.
30. Student tears one-half of one page of newspaper.
31. Student balls paper up in hand.
32. Student places paper in the left-hand corner of window.
33. Student pulls paper down to the bottom of window.
34. Student brings paper up to the top again.
35. Student places paper on the second fourth of window.
36. Student pulls paper down to the bottom of window.
37. Student brings paper to the top again.
38. Student places paper on the third fourth of window.
39. Student pulls paper down to the bottom of window.
40. Student brings paper up to the top right-hand corner of window.
41. Student pulls paper down to the bottom.
42. Student puts paper down beside pail.
43. Student washes and dries hands.

---

dividuals frequently lack the skills of imitation and incidental learning, and they do not generalize across settings or tasks readily. There are a number of methods for enhancing generalization, which are discussed in depth elsewhere (Wehman, Abramson, & Norman, 1977). Briefly, however, they include:

    a. varying the stimulus conditions of training, i.e., using different trainers and materials;

    b. including parents and peers in training;

    c. gradually fading reinforcement contingencies and substituting naturally occuring reinforcers;

d. training skills that have a high probability of
    being performed daily by the worker and are
    meaningful in content;
e. altering reinforcement schedules; and
f. developing self-control techniques, i.e., let-
    ting the trainee reinforce himself or herself

5. use of color coding, easy-to-hard sequencing, and
other learning variables that minimize failure are important
in helping students learn complex tasks; the trainer must
take the responsibility for the worker's inability to demonstrate proficiency on the job by making the task easier initially.

SOCIAL SKILLS IN VOCATIONAL SETTINGS

To this point, discussion has centered around training students to learn a skill and then perform it at an acceptable
rate. However, perhaps even more important, are the basic
social skills required in day-to-day living and contact with
other people. Examples of appropriate social behavior required on a job include shaking hands when introduced to
someone, greeting a peer, having a neat personal appearance, and getting to work on time.

Unfortunately, most severely handicapped workers do
not exhibit these social skills, and this prohibits their entry
into community workshops and labor forces. Gold (1973a)
notes:

> Whatever the reasons for the present status of the retarded,
> a wide discrepancy exists between what the retarded do,
> vocationally, and what they are potentially capable of doing
> both qualitatively and quantitatively. (p. 41)

A major reason for this wide discrepancy may be a
critical deficit that many severely handicapped workers

have in their social skill repertory. There are a number of skills that make up appropriate social behavior on the job and that pave the way to successful vocational adjustment. Learning and remembering social skills are necessary to keep a job. Time has shown, unfortunately, that those persons in society who behave "differently" may be stigmatized, excluded, and even feared. The severely developmentally disabled worker who is a steady worker but displays improper oral hygiene, fails to return friendly greetings, or cannot perform simple survival skills such as using the telephone, may be excluded by coworkers and eventually lose his job.

Rehabilitation counselors, workshop supervisors, and special educators face the increasing responsibility of training workers in social skills as well as establishing consistent task performance. The following section tries (1) to identify and delineate social skills required for successful vocational adjustment, (2) to arrange these skills into an hierarchical curriculum for training and evaluation, and (3) to suggest viable ways to implement the curriculum. Relevant and supportive empirical research is collated and synthesized as the underlying basis of the social skills curriculum. The curriculum is not intended to be wholly comprehensive. It should be viewed as representative of the adaptive behavior necessary for the occupational success of mentally handicapped workers.

A Social Skills Curriculum for Work Adjustment

The primary target population that the proposed social skills curriculum serves are moderately to profoundly handicapped workers. It is these persons who have the greatest social skill deficits and work adjustment needs.

The basic organizational structure of the social skills curriculum is delineated in four levels. Level 1 is the personal care level, which is made up of selected self-help skills. Level 2 is the primary interaction level, a level encompassing certain remedial communication skills. Level 3 consists of critical survival skills necessary to exist on the job. Level 4, the advanced interaction level, deals with the more subtle and sophisticated forms of human interaction, such as trust and cooperation. (Fig. 4–2) Several remarks should be made about interpreting the rationale behind the curriculum:

1. Skills are viewed as prerequisites to total vocational habilitation.
2. Skills are described behaviorally whenever possible.
3. An easy-to-hard learning sequence is established; that is, it is presumed that learning takes place more readily at the lower stages of the model.
4. Where appropriate, skills in the curriculum are broken into subcomponents and discussed.
5. The emphasis is not on the worker's level of retardation, but on the level of skill complexity that should initially be matched to a particular worker.

Personal Care—Level 1

Personal care forms the foundation of the social skills curriculum. The emphasis is on the finer self-help skills that directly affect how people will look at the worker. Toileting, simple dressing, and eating skills are presumed to be already in a person's repertoire. Proper table manners, one of the suggested personal care skills, can be subdivided into eating with the mouth closed; not talking with mouth full; not spilling food; using the proper utensils and napkin; and placing correct amount or portion on utensils.

Azrin and Armstrong (1973) demonstrated that profoundly retarded adults can learn neat eating habits within

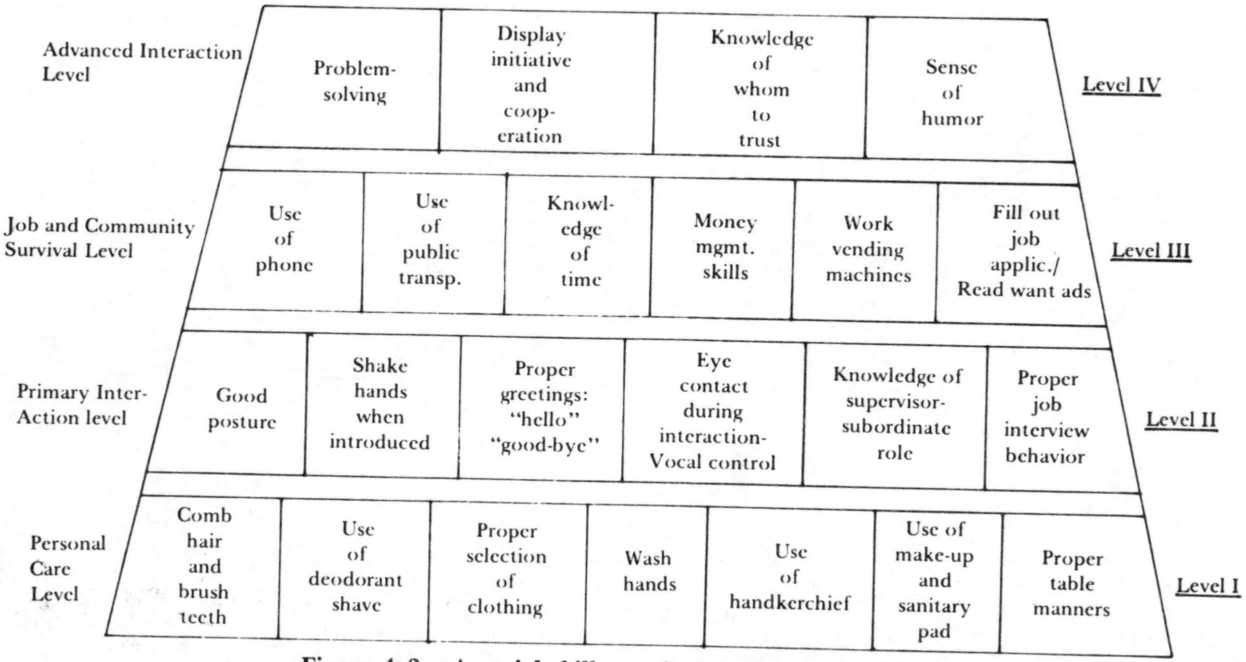

Figure 4-2. A social skills curriculum for handicapped workers in vocational settings.

several days by the "mini-meal" method of training. The "mini-meal" training method allows the person more chances to learn and practice correct eating habits. This is done through the presentation of several meals during the day instead of only three meals. The amount of food is the same as for three meals, but it is given in smaller portions over several meals during the day. The importance of neat eating habits cannot be minimized. During coffee breaks and lunch periods, the worker will be eating with coworkers daily. Poor eating habits can cast a negative reflection on the worker.

Dedrick (1974) presented a program for teaching severely handicapped adolescent females how to care for themselves during menstrual periods. She used a method of simulation during the training period. In training oral hygiene skills, Nietupski (1974) demonstrated a program to teach trainable adolescents how to use mouthwash. Successful acquisition and maintenance of grooming skills have also been demonstrated by Treffry, Martin, Samels, and Watson (1970) and by Wehman (1974). Cleanliness through proper oral hygiene is a vital social prerequisite to the vocational success that many retarded people can achieve but frequently fail to attain consistently. Prevocational training instructors must train workers in the need for daily hygiene maintenance.

Proper selection of clothing is another personal care skill that may have to be taught. The ability to dress oneself capably does not itself meet the stringent requirements of social acceptability. Some understanding of what clothing is appropriate for the job is required. Proper selection of clothing can be subdivided into several related clothing areas, and assessed in the following way: shoes on correct feet; fine motor dressing skills completed (e.g., zipping); shirt tucked in pants; clothes appropriate for work setting, jacket hung up properly every day; and clothes pressed and not wrinkled. The care and selection of clothing is important in job success, particularly in the initial stages when the worker must develop credibility.

It should be evident that the personal care level aims directly at the way a person looks. It may appear that the worker is being asked to conform too much, that he is losing his identity. This need not be the case. However, it must be recognized that society has set standards of social acceptance and success. For the severely developmentally disabled worker to succeed, he or she must conform to a certain level to establish credibility. The staff in sheltered workshops, halfway houses, and institutional workshops must take an active role in teaching and maintaining these skills. It seems that most workers can perform personal care skills with some degree of competence; however, the focus must be on maintaining and generalizing skills in different work settings.

Primary Interaction—Level 2

The primary interaction level also encompasses a range of behaviors which if absent, immediately alerts coworkers that there is something "wrong" with the worker. Eye contact during interaction and knowing when to interject one's comments into a conversation, for example, at coffee break, are extremely important subtleties largely taken for granted. It is usually natural to look at the person with whom one is talking. Unfortunately, many retarded workers do not do so, and they may mumble or not speak clearly because of articulation difficulties. Some workers may speak too loudly and not have an acceptable voice intensity.

These are social skills that have been trained to other retarded persons; behavior modification has been a successful teaching method. Voice intensity has been modified and generalized to other settings through the use of token reinforcement (Jackson & Wallace 1974). Attending behavior has been taught frequently to retarded persons and emotionally disturbed children (Walker & Buckley, 1968). The general procedure followed is reinforcement of each period of eye contact with the experimenter. In the situation mentioned above, the workshop supervisor would make reinforcement contingent on eye contact during interaction. Initially, verbal prompting might be required but could be faded as interactions became the discriminative stimuli for looking at the person being talked to.

Proper greetings of "hello" and "good-bye" are also social skills necessary for vocational development. Waving one's hand is an accepted practice of nonverbal greeting. In a recent study, Stokes, Baer, and Jackson (1974) trained severely handicapped children to use hand waving as a greeting response. Generalization of hand-waving was programmed across three different environments and four different experimenters.

Sitting up straight and walking with one's head up is another subtle social skill that reflects on a person. Workers should be encouraged to develop good posture at all times. O'Brien and Azrin (1970) demonstrated that posture can be taught and maintained in institution ward employees. It would appear that the same method of positive reinforcement procedures could be successful with mentally handicapped workers.

Another social skill that may in effect subsume much of the primary interaction level is proper job interveiw behavior. Many employers have varied stereotypes about what to expect when first meeting a retarded worker. The worker must be thoroughly trained by rehabilitation and education personnel in the necessary mechanics of a job interview. This means shaking hands, giving some form of greeting, maintaining eye contact, and responding to communication. The worker should also have some familiarity with the supervisor-subordinate relationship and understand who gives orders. It must be understood that only certain workers can tell him what to do and that he must sometimes accept constructive criticism.

The skills at the primary interaction level are not complex and are within the capabilities of many retarded people. Essentially they are those requiring somewhat more subtle discriminative cues. For example, the worker who is trained by rote to shake hands may do so only with those he is familiar with, or, alternatively, will offer his hand to people without an introduction. Similarly, a person who is taught to increase eye contact with peers may stare too much. Therefore it is important that the basic behavioral training principles of prompting, fading, reinforcement, and generalization are used carefully.

Job and Community Survival—Level 3

There are certain job and community survival skills which the severely developmentally disabled worker must acquire. However, many prerequisite behaviors and programs under each social skill category must be developed before the job and community survival level is fully attained.

Use of the telephone is definitely a survival skill. The retarded adult must be able to tell his or her supervisor of illness or inability to come to work. He or she must be able to ask for help if it is necessary to leave work and there is no ready transportation. Using a telephone effectively has been taught to trainable students by means of colors and numbers (Leff, 1974). Teaching use of the telephone is made up of at least three different subcomponents: reading the numbers 0 to 9; dialing numbers correctly; and making change correctly at pay phones. Each of these subcomponents may have to be further divided into smaller learning steps, depending on the behavioral level of the worker.

The severely developmentally disabled worker may have to take public transportation, such as a bus, train, or taxicab, to get to work. Certo and Schwartz (1975) have taught trainable adolescents to ride a bus in a medium-size midwestern city. Prerequisite skills included making change, knowing at which stop to get off, learning simple sight words, and telling time. Students were taught first through a videotaped simulation of various community bus routes. Gradually, students began taking real bus trips in the community without supervision.

The ability to fill out a job application correctly is an important part of the curriculum. This skill has been taught through task analysis to disadvantaged youths by Clark, Boyd, and MacCrae (1975).

Knowledge of time is another skill necessary for vocational success. The worker must be able to tell time for promptness. If his work shift changes, he must know the days of the week he is to work. Knowledge of time represents a number of skills depending on the dimension being taught. Learning calendar time involves reading the 7 days of the week, reading the 12 months of the year, and learning the sequence or cycle in which time occurs. Learning clock time involves reading the numbers 1 to 12 and discriminating the hour hand from the minute hand. Pierce (1972) was able to teach time-telling to trainable retarded students through task analysis.

Money management is another social skill necessary for success on the job. It includes behaviors such as counting and making change, cashing and depositing a paycheck into a bank account, working vending machines for food and drinks, and using the pay telephone. Money management skills require a series of prerequisite behaviors which, at the minimum, include sight word reading and simple arithmetic. Certo and Swetlik (1976) have developed an excellent functional money management program for severely handicapped students.

The job and community survival level encompasses a range of skills that require increasingly complex behaviors. Discriminative cues or signals for responding are even more subtle, and reinforcement is delayed. It is not expected that teachers and workshop professionals would spend long portions of the work period establishing social skills. Rather, it may be appropriate to pick one section of the job and community survival level and, in cooperation with the sponsoring social agency of the worker or parent, begin gradually to develop that skill in the worker.

Advanced Interaction—Level 4

The advanced interaction level includes cognitive-oriented skills, like problem solving, planning, trust, initiative, cooperation, and humor. These skills, also termed competence skills by Edmondson (1974), are high-level thought behaviors that are ultimately the link to "normalcy" or achieving personal independence. The influence of this skill group on vocational success and vocational opportunities should be obvious, particularly in the area of problem solving. The ability to think and to solve problems largely distinguishes intellect at all levels of normalcy and of retardation. Taking the initiative is frequently a function of how rapidly one is able to foresee where help is needed, and then having the confidence to intervene.

Knowing whom to trust and whom not to trust is a social skill many retarded people are deficient in. I was unable to locate any published reports of training an understanding of trust in mentally handicapped clients. Perske and Marquiss (1973) acknowledge that is a difficult concept for retarded adults who are being habilitated into the community.

> Live-in friends have provided specific training discussions on the proper use of the telephone, thermostat, medicine cabinet, garbage disposal, light switch, and so on. They must also teach their roommates how to deal with salesmen, taxicab drivers, and other community members. Learning whom to trust in the community is not an easy concept to grasp. (p. 18)

Demonstrating a sense of humor is a social behavior requiring more than bizarre laughing. Ellis (1973) discusses humor as defined by Berlyne:

> A cognitive process whereby a sequence of stimuli or ideas are strung together in such a way to generate an expectation which is shattered or a conflict which is suddenly resolved surprisingly. (p. 100)

The retarded person must know when to laugh and what is accepted as funny or not funny. Mentally handicapped people unquestionably have a sense of humor. The problem is that it may be socially misplaced or used at inappropriate times.

The advanced interaction level is a level where little supportive data-based research is available. Cognitive skills are more difficult to train and to generalize than are the concrete behaviors found at the personal care level. Although these skills are not critical to the success of the severely handicapped worker, they will certainly facilitate acceptance by coworkers.

METHODS OF IMPLEMENTING AND UTILIZING THE SOCIAL SKILLS CURRICULUM

Teachers and workshop supervisors should take an active role in teaching social skills as well as work skills. A worker who is functioning at a superior production level on the job, but who cannot get along with other workers, "acts out," doesn't want to be bothered, and so on, should be targeted for social skills training. Vocational training centers should hire additional personnel or convert positions to add social skill specialists who may monitor and train workers in social behaviors. It is granted that the purpose of a workshop is to attain production goals and to develop occupational expertise in workers. However, of what value is a skill if the worker cannot function socially with coworkers who may not be handicapped? For the severely handicapped worker to function in the least restrictive working environment, he or she must acquire basic social skills.

There are a number of possible administrative and clinical strategies for adapting the curriculum in a vocational setting. One suggested rehabilitation strategy is the behavioral approach depicted in the following five steps:

1. Initially assess all workers in the workshop on social skills curriculum. Use data and/or videotape for pretreatment evaluation, then find the level where the individual cannot function consistently.

2. Establish an instructional objective for each worker. Choose one skill at the designated level of the curriculum for each worker.

3. Select an appropriate training method. This may depend on the level of social skills at which the worker is functioning. At the lower levels, a behavior modification approach would be used. Levels 3 and 4 might require other teaching methods, most likely in combination. Such methods might be viewing a videotape, role playing, behavioral counseling, practice in decision making, and self-control procedures.

4. Every workday, spend a small portion of time in the general vocational setting, but removed from the work area, for training the worker in the target social skill.

5. Continue monitoring and recording data during training sessions. Make modifications in the program according to results.

This is one strategy, based on a functional analysis of behavior, that could be most successful in a rehabilitation setting. The extent and intensity of social skill programming in vocational training centers would be contingent on budget limitations and professional staff training.

Severely and profoundly handicapped workers have a strong need for social skill development in vocational settings. Social behavior is not the only factor that effects successful vocational experiences, but it is largely instrumental in helping workers adjust to the expectations of their employers. Rehabilitation professionals and teachers must play an increasingly active role in training workers in the social skills. More research should be directed at skills delineated in the curriculum, particularly in Levels 3 and 4. The curriculum presented in this chapter is an attempt to develop a training package for teaching social behavior. This tool can and should be modified for different settings. Only data-based programs can eventually verify the reliability and validity of the proposed curriculum.

CONVERTING ADULT DAYCARE PROGRAMS TO WORK ADJUSTMENT CENTERS

Many communities and counties are now providing adult daycare programs for moderately, severely, and profoundly handicapped adults. These programs usually do not directly address the work needs of severely handicapped individuals, but rather provide more of a recreational approach. It will be necessary to reallocate these resources and retrain personnel in the behavioral technology of vocational training.

A work adjustment program that can be used to help severely handicapped adults reach their full potential must involve the development of work habits and specific work skills, related social skills, and remedial training in self-help and language when trainees are clearly deficient. A series of planning and procedural steps is involved in establishing such a program. They are best completed if they are performed in a sequence and are carefully prepared beforehand. The steps below are provided as a programmatic and administrative sequence for moving an activity center more toward a work adjustment center.

Step One—Assess Physical Location

1. Is there at least one large room that can serve as a work center and several smaller rooms that can serve as training rooms?
2. Is there enough room so that trainees and staff are not cramped? Are windows and lighting adequate? Is there enough space for a break area and individualized rooms or cubicles for specialized training sessions?

Step Two—Establish Length of Workday

In this case, 9 AM to 3 PM would be appropriate, with time off for breaks, lunch, specific training classes in areas other than work skills, and field trips or swimming.

Step Three—Select Jobs or Tasks

1. Select jobs involving "sit-down tasks" relying on fine-motor skills, such as packaging, collating, and assembling.
2. Select jobs involving domestic or maintenance tasks relying on gross motor skills, such as making beds and washing dishes.
3. There should be a minimum of five of each tasks to start; they should be sequenced from easy to

hard in a range large enough to encompass most trainees' potential.

4. It should be understood that trainees will frequently be unable to demonstrate skills at first; they will have to be taught.

5. Tasks can be secured from other workshops and factories or generated by the staff. The tasks should be selected according to community needs and resources.

Step Four—Create a Work Environment Plan

1. Get a time clock and plan to teach trainees how to use it. This helps provide a signal for work.

2. Establish breaks and lunch periods.

3. Develop an incentive system to pay workers. (This should later be analyzed as a separate component.)

Step Five—Through Informal "Eyeball" Assessment, Place Trainees Into One of Three Skill Teams

1. Each staff member should be in charge of a work team and should have major input in developing trainees programs.

2. Teams may draw on the resources of college students or volunteers.

3. Teams should be grouped homogeneously in ability by physically placing them together at tables within the work area.

4. Trainees on teams should be able to move out of their team to the next higher team when they meet the work criteria requirements of the tasks assigned to that team.

5. The highest team members can be placed on a part-time basis in the community; State Dept of

Vocational Rehabilitation should help here. This lends itself to meeting the least restrictive environment mandate.

Step Six—Secure Task Raw Materials and Place them with Appropriate Teams

Step Seven—Assess Each Trainee on Task by Keeping Careful Records of Data

Use the task analysis method. For example, if there are 20 steps in a dishwashing task, assess over several days how many steps trainees in Team A can complete. Do this on all target tasks to help indicate the functioning level of the trainees.

Below is a sample sheet for dishwashing, which, if implemented, would be divided into many more steps. It may take 2 to 3 weeks to train workers in this task.

Steps	Independent	Needs Verbal Assistance	Needs Physical Assistance
1. Pick up dish			
2. Turn on water			
3. Pick up soap			

Step Eight—Begin Program

1. Decide which workers need training by analyzing the task assessment data.
2. Decide which workers can perform skills without training but need to work faster. Use the production strategies described earlier in this chapter.

VOCATIONAL OUTLOOK FOR SEVERELY HANDICAPPED WORKERS

The following conclusions about the vocational training potential of the severely retarded seem warranted.

1. Under appropriately arranged learning conditions, the severely retarded worker has the potential to perform reasonably complex manual tasks.
2. Supervision and training should be heaviest in the initial training stages, which may take at least 3 months, depending on task complexity. But as the task is acquired, supervision can be reduced substantially.
3. A significant problem in vocational programming for the severely retarded is the critical lack of appropriate social behavior. The inability to cope with frustrating events, bizarre verbal or motor behaviors, and basic social skill deficits all may contribute to rejection of the severely retarded individual as a successful employee.
4. Few studies demonstrate that the severely retarded are capable of competitive employment production rates; this is an area requiring investigation and one in which I am presently involved.

Although the work skill research reported in this chapter demonstrates the vocational behavior potential of severely retarded individuals, there are several issues, aside from social skill deficits, that may well prohibit their entry into community work forces. An initial problem is the probable reluctance of employers to take on severely retarded workers. There have been immense job placement problems with the mildly handicapped; certainly, acceptance of the severely retarded, a population with unique behavior characteristics, will be no easier.

Two potential avenues are open for overcoming this difficulty. Discrimination lawsuits or related litigation may alter employer's behavior, if not their attitudes. In addition, government subsidies may be temporarily directed to employers who are sympathetic to giving severely handicapped workers a chance to prove themselves.

Another issue that must be addressed by rehabilitation counselors is preparing trainees for the transition from the original training site to the least restrictive work environment, that is, a job placement in which the client can perform at his or her optimal level of independence. Most failures of vocational rehabilitation with developmentally disabled persons revolve around placement without proper preparation for the job. Role playing, similar work environments, behavior rehearsal, and gradual on-the-job training are ways of overcoming such failures. Volunteers and university practicum students may be used to assist busy rehabilitation counselors in this transition phase.

A final consideration in the eventual job placement of the severely retarded is the type of task or skill that they can perform. The complex assembly skill research reported here, although most impressive, is not all that practical. Many communities do not have any industry or need for workers who perform complex tasks. It may be wisest to train clients to meet the vocational needs of the community. Perusal of local newspaper job openings is one way to determine which skills should be taught.

The long-range outlook for severely retarded clients is presently equivocal. Rehabilitation professionals, with their broadbased training and service with many disabled populations, are in a position to help severely retarded persons adjust to vocational settings. However, vocational rehabilitation counselors must become familiar with behavior management techniques and accept this training technology. With these added skills, counselors can become even more effective in delivering vocational training and services.

REFERENCES

Azrin, N. H., & Armstrong, P. M. The "mini-meal"—A method for teaching eating skills to the profoundly retarded. *Mental Retardation,* January 1973, *11(1),* 9–13.

Azrin, N. H., Gottlieb, L., Hughart, L., Wesolowski, M. D., & Rahn, T. Eliminating self-injurious behavior by educative procedures. *Behavior Research and Therapy,* 1975, *13,* 101–111.

Bellamy, G. T. (Ed.). *Habilitation of severely and profoundly retarded adults.* Eugene, Oregon: University of Oregon, 1976.

Bellamy, G. T., Peterson, L., & Close, D. Habilitation of the severely and profoundly retarded: Illustrations of competence. *Education and Training of the Mentally Retarded,* 1975, *10,* 174–186.

Brown, L., & Pearce, E. Increasing the production rate of trainable retarded students in a public school simulated workshop. *Education and Training of the Mentally Retarded,* 1970, *5,* 15–22.

Brown, L., Bellamy. T. Perlmutter, L., Sackowitz, P. Sontag, E. The development of quantity, quality, and durability in the work performance of retarded students in a public school prevocational workshop. *Training School Bulletin,* 1972, *69,* 58–69.

Brown, L., Van Deventer, P., Perlmutter, L., Jones, S. & Sontag, E. Effects of consequences on production rates of trainable retarded and severely emotionally disturbed students in a public school workshop. *Education and Training of the Mentally Retarded,* 1972, *7,* 74–81.

Certo, N., & Schwartz, R. *Teaching trainable retarded students to ride a community bus.* Madison, Wisconsin: Department of Studies in Behavioral Disabilities, University of Wisconsin, 1975.

Certo, N., & Swetlik, B. Making purchases: A functional money use program for severely handicapped students. In L. Brown et al. (Eds.), *Madison's alternative to zero exclusion: Papers and programs related to public school services for secondary age severely handicapped students.* Madison, Wisconsin: Madison Public Schools, 1976.

Clark, H., Boyd, S., & MacCrae, S. A classroom program teaching disadvantaged youths to write biographic information *Journal of Applied Behavior Analysis,* 1975, *8(1),* 67–76.

Clarke, A., & Hermelin, F. Adult imbeciles: Their abilities and trainability. *The Lancet,* 1956, *2,* 337–339.

Crosson, J. A. technique for programming sheltered workshop environments for training severely retarded workers. *American Journal of Mental Deficiency,* 1969, *73,* 814–818.

Dedrick, P. Premenstrual training. In L. Brown, W. Williams & T. Crowner (Eds.), *A collection of papers and programs related to public school services for severely handicapped students.* Madison, Wisconsin: Madison Public Schools, 1974.

Edmondson, B. Arguing for a concept of competence. *Mental Retardation,* 1974, *12(6),* 14–15.

Ellis, M. J. *Why people play.* Englewood Cliffs, New Jersey: Prentice-Hall, 1973.

Gold, M. W. Stimulus factors in skill training of the retarded on a complex assembly task: Acquisition, transfer, and retention. *American Journal of Mental Deficiency,* 1972, *76,* 517–526.

Gold, M. W. Factors affecting production by the retarded: Base rate. *Mental Retardation,* 1973, *11(6),* 41–45 (a).

Gold, M. W. Research on the vocational habilitation of the retarded: The present, the future. In N. Ellis (Ed.), *International review of research in mental retardation* Vol. VI. New York: Academic Press, 1973 (b).

Gold, M. W. Redundant cue removal in skill training for the mildly and moderately retarded. *Education and Training of the Mentally Retarded,* 1974, *9,* 5–8.

Gold, M. W. Task analysis: A statement and an example using acquisition and production of a complex assembly task by the retarded blind. *Exceptional Children,* 1976, *43(2),* 78–87.

Gold, M. W., & Barclay, C. R. The learning of difficult visual discriminations by the moderately and severely retarded. *Mental Retardation,* 1973, *11,* 9–11.

Hollis, J. H. Development of perceptual motor skills in a profoundly retarded child. Part I. Prosthesis. *American Journal of Mental Deficiency,* 1967, *71,* 941–952. (a)

Hollis, J. H. Development of perceptual motor skills in a profoundly retarded child. Part II. Consequence, change, and transfer. *American Journal of Mental Deficiency,* 1967, *71,* 953–963. (b)

Hunter, J., & Bellamy, G. T. Cable harness construction for severely retarded adults: A demonstration of training techniques. *AAESPH Review,* 1976, *1(7),* 2–13.

Irvin, L. General utility of easy-to-hard discrimination training procedures with the severely retarded. *Education and Training of the Mentally Retarded,* 1976, *11(3),* 247–250.

Irvin, L., & Bellamy, G. T. Manipulation of stimulus features in vocational skill training of the severely retarded: Relative efficacy. *American Journal of Mental Deficiency,* 1977, *81(2).*

Jackson, D. A., & Wallace, R. F. The modification and generalization of voice loudness in a fifteen-year-old girl. *Journal of Applied Behavior Analysis,* 1974, *7(3),* 461–472.

Karan, O. C., Wehman, P., Renzaglia, A., & Schutz, R. *Habilitation practices with the severely developmentally disabled.* University of Wisconsin: Rehabilitation Research and Training Center, 1976.

Kazdin, A. E. The effect of response cost and aversive stimulation in suppressing punished and nonpunished speech disfluencies. *Behavior Therapy,* 1973, *4,* 73–82.

Kliebhahn, J. Effects of goal setting and modeling on job performances of retarded adolescents. *American Journal of Mental Deficiency,* 1967, *72,* 220–226.

Leff, Ruth B. Training the TMR to dial the telephone. *Mental Retardation,* 1974, *12(2),* 12–13.

Madsen, C., Becker, W., Thomas, D., Koser, L., & Plager, E. An analysis of the reinforcing function of "sit-down" commands. In R. K. Parker (Ed.), *Readings in educational psychology.* Boston: Allyn and Bacon, 1970, 265–278.

MacDonough, T. & Forehand, R. Response-contingent time-out: Important parameters in behavior modification with children. *Journal of Behavior Therapy and Experimental Psychiatry,* 1973, *4,* 231–236.

Nietupski, R. Use of mouthwash. In L. Brown, W. Williams, & T. Crowner (Eds.), *A collection of papers and programs related to public school services for severely handicapped students.* Madison, Wisconsin: Madison Public Schools, 1974.

O'Brien, F., & Azrin, N. H. Behavioral engineering: Control of posture by informational feedback. *Journal of Applied Behavior Analysis,* 1970, *3(4),* 235–240.

Perske, R., & Marquis, J. Learning to live in an apartment: Retarded adults from institutions and dedicated citizens. *Mental Retardation,* 1973, *11(5),* 18–19.

Pierce, L. Teaching time-telling. In L. Brown & E. Sontag (Eds.), *Toward the development and implementation of an empiricially based public school program for trainable mentally retarded and severely emotionally disturbed students.* Madison, Wisconsin: Madison Public Schools, 1972.

Renzaglia, A., Wehman, P., Schutz, R., & Karan, O. Use of cue redundancy and positive reinforcement to accelerate production rates in two profoundly retarded workers. *British Journal of Social and Clinical Psychology,* 1978, *17(2).*

Rusch, F., & Close, D. Overcorrection: A procedural evaluation. *AAESPH Review,* 1976, *1(5),* 32–45.

Schroeder, S. Parametric effects of reinforcement frequency, amount of reinforcement, and required response force on sheltered workshop behavior. *Journal of Applied Behavior Analysis,* 1972, *5,* 431–441.

Schutz, R., Wehman, P., Renzaglia, A., & Karan, O. Efficacy of contingent social disapproval on inappropriate verbalizations of two severely retarded males. *Behavior Therapy,* in press.

Stokes, T. F., Baer, D. M., & Jackson, R. L. Programming the generalization of a greeting response in four retarded children. *Journal of Applied Behavior Analysis,* 1974, *7(4),* 599–610.

Tobias, J., & Gorelick, J. The effectiveness of the Purdue Pegboard in evaluating the work potential of retarded adults. *Training School Bulletin,* 1963, *57,* 94–103.

Treffry, D., Martin, G., Samels, K., & Watson, P. Operant conditioning of grooming behavior of severely retarded girls. *Mental Retardation,* August 1970, *8(4),* 29–33.

Walker, H., & Buckley, N. The use of positive reinforcement in conditioning attending behavior. *Journal of Applied Behavior Analysis,* 1968, *1,* 245–250.

Wehman, P. Maintaining oral hygiene skills in geriatric retarded women. *Mental Retardation,* 1974, *12(4),* 20.

Wehman, P., Abramson, M., & Norman, C. Transfer of training in behavior modification programs: an evaluative review. *Journal of Special Education,* 1977, *11(2),* 217–231.

Wehman, P., Renzaglia, A., Schutz, R., & Karan, O. Stimulating productivity in two profoundly retarded workers through mixed reinforcement contingencies. In O. Karan, P. Wehman, A. Renzaglia, & R. Schutz (Eds.), *Habilitation practices with the severely developmentally disabled.* Madison, Wisconsin: University of Wisconsin Rehabilitation Research and Training Center, 1976.

Wehman, P., Schutz, R., Bates, P., Renzaglia, A., & Karan, O. Self-management programs with mentally retarded workers: Implications for developing independent vocational behavior. *British Journal of Social and Clinical Psychology,* 1978, *17(1),* 58–68.

Wehman, P., Schutz, R., Renzaglia, A., & Karan, O. Use of positive practice to facilitate increased work productivity and instruction following in profoundly retarded adolescents. *Vocational Evaluation and Work Adjustment,* 1977, *10(3,)* 14–19.

Williams, P. Industrial training and remunerative employment of the profoundly retarded. *Journal of Mental Subnormality,* 1967, *13,* 14–23.

Zimmerman, J., Overpeck, C., Eisenberg, H., & Garlick, B. Operant conditioning in a sheltered workshop. *Rehabilitation Literature,* 1969, *30,* 323–334.

Chapter 5

MOTOR DEVELOPMENT

Most severely and profoundly handicapped individuals are deficient in some aspect of gross and fine motor development. Young severely handicapped children fail to explore and move about in the environment and thus reduce sensory awareness and incidental learning. Failure to acquire these behaviors impedes the development of many adaptive behaviors and also precludes advances in preacademic skills. Independent ambulation is clearly a cornerstone of self-sufficient behavior and must be considered a critical area of learning for the severely handicapped (Stainback & Stainback, 1976).

Grossly delayed motor behavior may be a result of organic or structural brain damage, as with cerebral palsy, or it may simply be a behavioral characteristic of profound mental retardation. Obviously, procedures for ameliorating such motor deficiencies are more promising with the profoundly retarded since they are not constrained by physiological limitations on motor development.

Sensory-Motor Stimulation and Patterning

Numerous programs have been directed at overcoming motor deficits, many of which have emphasized the crucial role of movement and stimulation (e.g., Bradley, Konicki, & Leedy, 1968). These studies have been characterized by the work of major perceptual motor theorists such as Kephart (1960), Frostig (1972), the Bobaths (1971), and Doman and Delacato (LeWinn, Doman, Delacato, Doman, Spitz, & Thomas, 1966). Much of this research is based on the tenet that movement and planned sensory stimulation result in greater motor development.

Webb (1969) formulated one such program based on an excellent set of training procedures, and an assessment device based on the sensory-motor stages of development described by Piaget (1951). This test, which was standardized on profoundly retarded children, includes 75 test items in the areas of awareness, manipulation, and posture development. A separate manual for training, test administration, and scoring is also available. The greatest strength of Webb's work lies in the development of training procedures that are specific to certain areas of motor deficiencies. Table 5–1 gives an abbreviated version of the awareness, manipulation, and posture index.

Another study which examined the effects of sensory-motor training on adaptive behavior was reported by Edgar (1969). A group of children who received sensory-motor training made significant gains on the Gesell development schedule compared to children in a control group who received personal attention only. Training was performed in 8 months.

Sensory-motor patterning has also been used to improve motor skills in trainable retarded children (Neman, Roos, McCann, Menolascino, & Heal, 1975). This study compared three groups of subjects. Two experimental groups were utilized, one which received the Doman-

Table 5–1. AMP Index No. 1 (Seventh Revision)

Name _____   Date Rated _____ _____ _____

Case No. _____   Evaluator _____ _____ _____

                                  Observer _____ _____ _____

Total Awareness Score _____ _____ _____

Total Manipulation Score _____ _____ _____

Total Posture Score
(Static and Dynamic) _____ _____ _____

Awareness Index _____ _____ _____

Manipulation Index _____ _____ _____

Posture Index _____ _____ _____

Total AMP Index _____ _____ _____

Total AMP Index	1	/	2	/	3
	0–75		76–150		151–225

(The number above the range interval into which the Total AMP Index score falls is the Total AMP Index.)

Directions: Please rate the frequency of the action responses in capital letters on the scale following each item. If the item contains two or more stimulus words (in parentheses), underline the appropriate stimulus words. Items should be rated for responses only during the testing period. For instructions in giving the individual items, please consult the manual.

Rating System: Opposite each item are five columns (see below). They are headed "0," "1," "2," "3," and "Total." Present each item three times. If the child responds to the item each time you present it check "3." If the child responds twice, check "2," and if once, check "1." If the child makes no response at all, check "0."

0	1	2	3	Total

The index for each section is found by adding the ratings for all items in the section and locating the total on the scale that follows each part of the AMP. The number on the scale above the total score is the index for the individual AMP section. The score and index for the complete AMP are found in a similar way: add the scores for all parts of the AMP and locate the sum on the scale at the top of this page. The number above the score for the total AMP is the index for the total AMP.

More than one column for the scores and indices is provided on the front page so that each form may be used at least three times. It is suggested that ratings at different times be marked with different colored pens: green, red, and blue. BE SURE TO NOTE THE DATE EACH TIME YOU USE THE FORM. A TEST IS USELESS WITHOUT THE DATE. Each time you use the form, be sure both the child's name and your name are on it.

By Ruth C. Webb, Ph.D., Director of Developmental Therapy, Glenwood State Hospital School, Glenwood, Iowa 51534

Name _____ Case No. _____

AWARENESS

Note: Sensory systems are designated by the abbreviations following each item: T—Tactility (Te—Temperature and P—Pain), K—Kinesthesia, V—Vision, A—Audition, G—Gustatory, O—Olfactory, Me—Memory, and At—Attention.

0	1	2	3	Total

A. *Avoidance:*
1. STRUGGLES when held tightly (T, Pr)
2. DRAWS wrist or knee away from sharp tapping from rubber hammer (underline) (T, P)
3. DRAWS cheek away from sandpaper (T, P)
4. DRAWS right and left hands out of hot water (120° F) and cold water (40° F) (underline) (T, Te)
5. JUMPS or BLINKS eyes when metal basin is dropped 2 feet behind child (underline) (K, A)
6. TURNS away from strong light (V)

153

Table 5-1. (Continued)

	0	1	2	3	Total

7. DRAWS away from unpleasant odors: A, potassium sulphate; B, turpentine (O)

8. DRAWS away from unpleasant tastes: A, lemon; B, salt; C, alum (G)

9. STRUGGLES to regain upright position (3–6 months) (K)

B. *Approach:*

10. DRAWS closer or SMILES when cuddled (underline (T)

11. MAINTAINS CONTACT with or PATS pliable materials for 10 seconds: A, sand; B, wet clay; C, water (underline) (T)

12. SMILES or TURNS toward bell (underline) (A)

13. SMILES, TURNS, or REACHES toward music (underline) (A)

14. SMILES when evaluator smiles (social response) (V)

15. TURNS toward hanging ball (V)

16. TURNS toward voice from behind (A)

17. REACHES toward pleasant odors: A, Charisma perfume; B, oil of lemon; C, oil of cinnamon (underline) (O)

18. REACHES toward pleasant taste: sugar or sugar water (underline) (G)

C. *Integrating Memory with Present Stimuli:*

19. LOOKS at familiar person when named (A, V, Me) _____

20. OBEYS gesture command (raises arms in response to outstretched arms) (V, Me) _____

21. LOOKS in direction of a block that has been dropped (V, A, Me) _____

22. TURNS head or SMILES when name is called (underline) (A, Me) _____

23. SHIFTS attention from one toy to another (V, A, At) _____

24. TURNS toward objects as they are named (ball, spoon) (underline) (A, V, Me) _____

25. REACTS to reappearance of evaluator (V, A, Me) _____

Total AWARENESS Score _____

Awareness Index	1	/	2	/	3
	0–25		26–50		51–75

(The number above the range interval into which the Total AWARE-NESS Score falls is the AWARENESS Index. Please place the Total AWARENESS Score and the AWARENESS Index in the appropriate spaces on page 1.)

Name _____ Case No. _____

MANIPULATION

Note: In addition to the sensory systems designated in the AWARENESS Scale, the MANIPULATION Scale includes: GM—Gross Motor, FM—Fine Motor, I—Imitation, PP—Person Permanence, Int—Intentionality, Comm—Communications, and OP—Object Permanence.

0	1	2	3	Total

Table 5–1. (Continued)

Name _____ Case No. _____

	0	1	2	3	Total

A. *Responses to Objects:*
    26. REACHES for object with right, left, or both hands (V, At, FM, Int) (underline)
    27. GRASPS object with right, left, or both hands (V, FM, Int) (underline)
    28. HOLDS object with right, left, or both hands (V, A, FM, Int) (underline)
    29. TRANSFERS toy from hand to hand (V, T, FM, Int)
    30. SQUEEZES ball (T, I, FM, Int)

B. *Responses to Commands:*
Gestures:
    31. POUNDS table with block (V, T, A, I, FM, Int)
    32. PICKS up bead with finger and thumb (V, T, I, FM, Int)
    33. DROPS block in can (V, A, I, FM, Int)
    34. PUTS ring on stick (V, I, T, FM, Int)
    35. POURS sand or water from one can to another (V, T, I, FM, Int) (underline)
    36. IMITATES poking finger into hole (V, I, T, Int)
    37. PLAYS peek-a-boo (I, A, PP, Int)
    38. PAT-A-CAKES (V, I, A, Int)

Words:

39. In sitting position, PULLS toy across table toward self with string (V, FM, A, Int) _____

40. REMOVES box covering candy (V, OP, A, Int) _____

41. THROWS ball purposely (A, V, Int) _____

42. STACKS one block on another (A, Int) _____

43. SCRIBBLES on paper (A, FM, Int) _____

44. OBEYS verbal command ("Give me your hand.") (A, Int) _____

C. *Expression of Intentionality:*

45. EXPRESSES need by: (1) sounds; (2) eyes; (3) gestures; (4) words (underline) (V, A, Int, Comm) _____

46. REMOVES towel from head (active avoidance) (V, FM, Int) _____

47. PATS mirror image (V, T, Int) _____

48. PULLS evaluator's arm to get balloon (V, FM, Int) _____

49. PULLS evaluator's arm to indicate choice of toy (V, A, Int, Comm) _____

50. RESISTS when treat is taken away (V, Int, Comm) _____

Total MANIPULATION Score _____

Manipulation Index	1	/	2	/	3
	0–25		26–50		51–75

Table 5-1. (Continued)

(The number above the range interval into which the Total MANIPULA-TION Score falls is the MANIPULATION Index. Please place the Total MANIPULATION Score and the MANIPULATION Index in the appropriate spaces on page 1.)

Name _____ Case No. _____

POSTURE (Static and Dynamic)

Note: In this section, S for Static and D for Dynamic are shown in parentheses after each item. If the child walks with assistance, rate starred (*) items 51-55, 57-60, 62, 64-71 with "3."

	0	1	2	3	Total
51. *HOLDS up head for at least 1 minute (S)					
52. *ROLLS from stomach to back or from back to stomach (D)					
53. *ROLLS completely over (D)					
54. *MOVES on back purposely by pushing arms or legs (underline) (D)					
55. *MOVES on stomach purposely by pivoting arms and legs (D)					
56. GIVES ACTIVE ASSISTANCE when limbs are moved in reciprocal pattern (D)					
57. *SITS without support for 1 minute (S)					
58. *MOVES on seat (D)					
59. *MOVES forward on stomach by pushing with arms or legs or both (D)					
60. *CREEPS by moving arms and legs bilaterally (D)					
61. STANDS on hands and knees (S)					

62. *CRAWLS bilaterally (D) _____

63. CRAWLS translaterally (D) _____

64. *PULLS to stand on knees
(D) _____

65. *PULLS to stand on feet (D) _____

66. *STANDS supported in
standing table for at least 1
minute (S) _____

Name _____ Case No. _____

0	1	2	3	Total

67. *STANDS holding chair at
least 1 minute (S) _____

68. *STANDS holding adult's
hand at least 1 minute (S) _____

69. *STANDS unsupported at
least 1 minute (S) _____

70. *WALKS with one hand held
for at least 10 feet (D) _____

71. *WALKS with pushcart at
least 10 feet (D) _____

72. WALKS alone at least 10 feet
(D) _____

73. ROCKS in a chair at least
three times (D) _____

74. BOUNCES on bed or trampoline at least three times (D) _____

75. MAINTAINS sitting position
on balance board for at least
three rocks (S) _____

Total POSTURE Score _____

Posture Index _____ 1 ____ / ___ 2 ___ / ___ 3 _____
　　　　　　　　0–25　　　　　26–50　　　　51–75

(The number above the range interval into which the Total POSTURE
Score falls is the POSTURE Index. Please place the Total POSTURE
Score and the POSTURE Index in the appropriate spaces on page 1.)

Reprinted with the kind permission of Ruth Webb, Ph.D.

Delacato method of patterning and mobility exercises, and the other which received similar levels of physical activity and personal attention. A passive control group provided baseline measures for the experimental manipulation.

Each subject in the patterning group received four 5-minute patterning sessions in every 30 minutes in a 2-hour time period. The program lasted approximately 6 months. Results indicated that the experimental group that received sensory motor patterning made the greatest gains in motor development. Although some have criticized this study on methodological grounds (Zigler & Seitz, 1975), it appears to be logically sound and of clinical value.

Of course, the cost and manpower involved in much of this research may preclude complete implementation of these programs in classrooms. One-to-one ratios between staff and subjects, expensive equipment, and many staff hours were spent in making motor development gains. The practical utility of these methods in special education classrooms with one teacher and an aide remains a logistical question.

BEHAVIOR MODIFICATION TECHNIQUES

Behavioral training procedures have also been used in overcoming motor deficits in the severely and profoundly handicapped. Task analysis, use of developmental norms for assessment, and systematically applied reinforcement contingencies characterize the methodology utilized to shape motor behavior.

Adaptive physical education methods have been combined with a behavior modification approach to motor development (Auxter, 1971). Increasing range of motion, development of extensor strength, proprioceptive stimulation, and integrative function of joints were target areas identified for training 12 nonambulatory, profoundly retarded adolescents. Candy was used to reinforce appropriate motor skills. Auxter reported difficulty in eliciting the target behaviors because subjects were exceptionally withdrawn and unwilling to engage in increased motor activity. Positive gains were made, although the extent of the improvement was not stated.

Physical education programs have been employed in improving the physical fitness and muscle tone of trainable retarded boys (Campbell, 1974). The Royal Canadian Air Force Physical Fitness Training Program was carried out with an experimental and control group. In the experimental group, principles of contingency management were applied during training. Subsequent results indicated greater gains in the experimental group. Profoundly retarded males have also been trained to do sit-ups, push-ups, and duckwalking through task analysis, backward chaining, and social reinforcement (Wehman, Renzaglia, Berry, Schutz, & Karan, 1978).

Numerous other programs demonstrate the effectiveness of an operant conditioning approach in the development of ambulation (Loynd & Barclay, 1970; Macaulay & MacMillan, 1970; Wilson & Parks, 1970). One such report describes the efficacy of contingent music on the independent walking of an 8-year-old severely retarded boy with special health problems (Chandler & Adams, 1972). In this program the number of steps taken independently was measured as the outcome variable, and results were evaluated in a baseline-treatment (AB) design. The training period lasted 28 days. In similar studies multiply handicapped children learned to use crutches (Horner, 1971) and a wheelchair (Grove, 1976).

Rice and his colleagues have also successfully applied behavioral principles to establishing sensory awareness and arm-hand movement to the nonambulatory profoundly retarded (Rice, McDaniel, Stallings, & Gatz, 1967; Rice & McDaniel, 1966). The latter study exemplified the influence of reinforcement and shaping through successive approximations. The frequency of interaction with rattle toys by a 6-year-old profoundly retarded child was substantially increased.

Perhaps the most extensive research completed with nonambulatory profoundly mentally retarded (NPMR) individuals is reported by Landesman-Dwyer and Sackett (1975). These investigators reviewed relevant research in this area and reported a 12-month observational study of NPMR children. NPMR children were defined according to the following criteria (Landesman-Dwyer & Sackett, 1975, p. 37):

1. Extremely limited or no apparent responses to external stimulation
2. Obvious, severe neuromuscular dysfunction
3. Inability to move through space by any means other than simple turning
4. Inability to achieve or maintain a seated position
5. Poor head control
6. Abnormally small body size for chronological age
7. Institutional records indicating a "hopeless" prognosis for behavioral and physiological development, even with treatment

The research carried out by Fuller (1949), Rice (Rice & McDaniel, 1966; Rice, McDaniel, Stallings, & Gatz, 1967), Goshgorian (1968), Lederman (1969), and Piper and Mackinnon (1969) demonstrates that NPMR individuals can acquire simple motor behaviors such as increased arm movements, greater "looking" behavior, and increased body extension. From the research studies cited above, Landesman-Dwyer and Sackett (1975, p. 39) drew the following conclusions about NPMR behavior:

1. Relative to normal and higher level retarded children, NPMR subjects have an *extremely limited repertoire of behaviors* judged suitable for conditioning.

2. NPMR children have *remarkably low baseline operant rates* for those behaviors judged suitable for conditioning, often as low as two or three per hour.

3. For many NPMR subjects, *extensive shaping of a response or eliciting of orienting responses* is essential, before operant techniques can be applied effectively;

4. "It is necessary to have a *wide variety of potentially reinforcing* stimuli available for testing, and to expect the effect to be unpredictable as compared to normal and higher grade retardates" (Rice & McDaniel, 1966, p. 280). For example, food deprivation often has no effect on rate of conditioning in NPMR subjects.

5. Frequently, NPMR children *demonstrate behaviors not anticipated* or knowingly controlled by the experimenter, e.g., increasingly accurate movements in reaching for an object; smiling vocalizing, orienting toward a stimulus; or showing signs of recognizing the experimenter.

6. NPMR children tend to have highly variable response rates, even after conditioning has been reliably demonstrated. For reasons not clearly delineated, there are very long inter-response intervals.

7. Many NPMR subjects demonstrate a phenome-
non labeled *spontaneous extinction* (Rice & McDaniel, 1966) after considerable exposure to the
conditioning paradigm. This spontaneous extinction is characterized by a sudden decline in or
cessation of responding, although no known
changes in the experimental procedure have occurred. To date, published attempts to re-estab-
lish responding in such subjects have failed
miserably, regardless of the reinforcing stimuli
or schedules of reinforcement.

Through use of a complex observational coding system, Landesman-Dwyer (1974) documented the positive
effects which different experimental "enrichment" conditions had on several dependent measures in NPMR children. The three treatment conditions involved (1)
placement in a playpen alone for 30 minutes, (2) placement
in a playpen with four to eight toys presented by the experimenter for 30 minutes, and (3) placement in a playpen with
a peer placed across from the child for 30 minutes. As
might be expected, the latter two conditions resulted in the
greatest changes in the children. During treatment in the
playpens, and on the ward, the following behavioral areas
showed the greatest change (Landesman-Dwyer & Sackett,
1975, p. 58):

1. Increased contacts with the environment or with
   peers
2. Increased "looking" behaviors
3. Increased head control
4. Increased facial expressiveness
5. Decreased mouthing behaviors
6. Decreased fixed action sequences

7.   More complex behavioral profiles, with new behaviors emerging

Curriculum Sequences

There is little doubt that the most outstanding work in this
area is in recent curriculum development strategies developed by Diane Bricker and her associates at the University
of Miami (e.g., Bricker, Davis, Wahlin, & Evans, 1976), and
in the instructional program and teaching procedures provided by Brown, Scheuerman, and Crowner in Madison,
Wisconsin (1976). In the motor training program developed by Bricker, a developmental sequence of reflexive
behavior, head, trunk, and limb control, coordination and
balance, manual dexterity, and locomotion and agility is
outlined along with suggested activities and teaching strategies. In the motor program developed by Brown and his
coworkers, instructional sequences and strategies for obstacle course skills, handwalking, and head control are generated. Tracking and scanning skill programs are also
available for the nonambulatory profoundly handicapped
child. For an indepth discussion of methods and techniques
on handling and positioning the severely physically involved child, the reader is referred to the work of Utley,
Holvoet, and Barnes (1977).

As an illustration of a fine motor instructional sequence, consider the program outlined below. In this program, specific fine motor skills are sequenced. Each skill is
taught or mediated through activities. One way in which
this program could be strengthened would be by adding
other, more creative activities. Through the precise delineation of child and teacher behaviors expected, the program has a greater likelihood of being replicated by other
less experienced teachers.

A Sample Fine Motor Program for
Profoundly Handicapped Children[1]

1. *Reaching, grasping, and retaining*

   Objective: The student will reach purposefully with dominant and nondominant hand for an object 12 inches from the body, grasp it, and retain it with a palmar grasp for 10 seconds.

   Prerequisites: attending to instructions
   ability to open hand
   ability to maintain eye contact with object

   Materials: noise-making object, e.g., bell with handle
   towel for tug-of-war
   weight to immobilize hand not being used

   Activity I Cue: "Hold the bell."

   A. Dominant hand

Student behaviors	*Teacher behaviors*
1. S reaches for object directly by and nearly touching hand	a) T shows S bell, demonstrates noise, places bell by S's hand
	b) T gives verbal cue, waits 5 seconds; if S responds correctly, T reinforces
	c) T repeats verbal cue; if S responds correctly, T reinforces
	d) T models behavior
	e) T repeats verbal cue; if S responds correctly, T reinforces (gains S's eye contact by holding reinforcer in front of his eyes, then moves reinforcer next to bell)
	f) T physically prompts by taking S's hand and moving it to touch bell; T reinforces
2. S grasps object directly by and nearly touching hand a) S touches object b) S opens hand	a) T places bell directly by S's hand b) T gives verbal cue, waits 5 seconds; if S responds correctly, T reinforces

166

c) *S* closes hand around object
d) *S* maintains grasp for:
   2 seconds
   4 seconds
   6 seconds
   10 seconds

c) *T* repeats verbal cue; if *S* responds correctly, *T* reinforces
d) *T* models behavior
e) *T* repeats verbal cue; if *S* responds correctly, *T* reinforces
f) *T* physically prompts by:
   1) placing slight pressure with one finger on *S*'s elbow
   2) moving *S*'s hand to bell
   3) opening *S*'s hand
   4) placing bell in *S*'s hand
   5) closing hand over *S*'s to ensure grasp
   6) reinforce

3. Repeat steps 1 and 2 with the object moved successively to:
   2 inches from *S*
   4 inches from *S*
   6 inches from *S*
   8 inches from *S*
   10 inches from *S*
   12 inches from *S*

B. Nondominant hand

Follow the same sequence used with the dominant hand.

Pair primary and social reinforcement. As *S*'s response becomes fairly consistent after teacher behavior b) or c), gradually reduce primary reinforcement to every third trial, but maintain social reinforcement. Using a weight to immobilize the hand not being used may prove helpful.

Activity II Cue: "Hold the towel."

Student behaviors	*Teacher behaviors*
Same as for Activity I	Same as for Activity I. To promote grasp maintenance, *T* can hold opposite end of towel and gently pull while repeating cue. Made into a game, this may motivate the student. Modeling with another student may be

helpful. Exaggerated facial expression and tone of voice in the
game situation may be helpful
variables.

2. *Picking up object*

Objective: The student will lift hand and arm completely off any
supporting surface while maintaining grasp on an object,
and will maintain this lift with dominant and nondominant hands for 10 seconds.

Materials: ridged ball (6 inches or more in diameter)
sand sieve, sand, and container

Activity I Cue: "Pick up the ball."

A. Dominant hand

Student behaviors	*Teacher behaviors*
1. S touches object	a) T shows S ball, demonstrates
2. S grasps object (pal-	action of picking up ball
mar grasp)	while pairing verbal cue
3. S picks up object by	"Pick up the ball."
lifting hand off surface	b) T places ball by S's hand
4. S picks up object by	c) T gives verbal cue, waits 5
lifting hand and arm	seconds; if S responds cor-
off surface	rectly, T reinforces
5. S completes step 4	d) T repeats verbal cue; if S
maintaining lift and	responds correctly, reinforce
grasp for:	e) T models behavior
2 seconds	f) T repeats verbal cue; if S
4 seconds	responds correctly, reinforce
6 seconds	g) T physically prompts by:
10 seconds	1) moving S's hand to
	touch ball
	2) placing ball in S's hand
	3) applying slight pressure
	with one finger on S's
	elbow
	4) applying slight pressure
	under S's hand
	5) lifting S's hand off sup-
	porting surface
	6) lifting S's arm off sup-
	porting surface
	7) reinforcing

B.   Nondominant hand

Repeat the same sequence used with the dominant hand.

Pair primary and social reinforcement. As *S*'s response becomes fairly consistent after teacher behavior c) or d), gradually reduce primary reinforcer to every third trial, but maintain social reinforcement.

Activity II Cue: "Pick up the sieve."

Student behaviors	*Teacher behaviors*
Same as for Activity I	Same as for Activity I. Container with sand should be large enough in area to permit free movement of sieve, and the container's sides should be only 3–4 inches high, so the student can easily see over the sides and have easy access to the sand and sieve. The sieve should ideally have a handle and holes large enough to allow easy flow of sand so that *S* is not required to shake the sieve to make the sand fall. Primary reinforcement may be faded as the activity of watching the sand becomes reinforcing by itself. Interaction of *T* with *S* in a play situation using a second sieve and modeling techniques can be effective in promoting motivation and mastery. The instructional setting should vary from classroom to playground sandbox and *S* should be placed in different positions: sitting in a chair, standing on the floor, etc.

3.   *Squeezing soft toys*

Objective: When given a soft toy, the student will squeeze it by alternately opening and closing fingers 5 times in 10 seconds with dominant and nondominant hands.

Materials: playdough

Activity I Cue: "Squeeze it."

A. Dominant hand

Student behaviors	*Teacher behaviors*
1. *S* grasps playdough when handed to him	a) *T* demonstrates squeezing playdough
2. *S* squeezes playdough by closing and opening fingers: once in 10 seconds twice in 10 seconds 3 times in 10 seconds 4 times in 10 seconds 5 times in 10 seconds	b) *T* puts playdough in *S*'s hand and lets him feel it; squeezes his fingers into dough a few times c) *T* hands playdough to *S* d) *T* gives verbal cue; waits 5 seconds; if *S* responds correctly, *T* reinforces e) *T* repeats verbal cue; if *S* responds correctly, reinforces f) *T* models behavior with another ball of playdough g) *T* repeats verbal cue; if *S* responds correctly, *T* reinforces h) *T* physically prompts by: 1) rubbing inside of *S*'s wrist 2) rubbing back of hand 3) placing *T*'s hand over *S*'s and squeezing fingers in required manipulation 4) reinforcing

B. Nondominant hand

Repeat same sequence used with dominant hand.

Pair primary and social reinforcement. As *S*'s response becomes fairly consistent after teacher behaviors d) and e), gradually reduce primary reinforcement to every third trial, but maintain social reinforcement.

If *S* completes one or so open-close squeezes, but fails to perform the criterion of 5 in 10 seconds, repeating the verbal cue after each squeeze may be necessary along with reinforcing first after one squeeze, then only after 2 squeezes, then after 3, etc., until criterion has been reached.

Other suggested activities

a) flexible squeaking toy
b) squeeze-type flour or sand sifter
c) sponge in water
d) meat baster in water (colored for motivation)

Instructional settings should change where appropriate. Use activities in as natural a setting as possible.

4. *Pats, slaps, pushes against*

Objective: Having made hand contact with an object 10 inches in front of her, student will exert opposing force on object with hand to move the object away from her body with both dominant and nondominant hands.

Materials: toy with suction bottom
water tray
balloon
large ball

Activity I Cue: "Hit the toy."

The student should be standing or sitting behind table. Suction bottom toy is placed on table 10 inches in front of S.

A. Dominant hand

Student behaviors

1. S reaches for toy
2. S opens hand
3. S touches toy with palm of hand
4. S pushes against toy
5. S withdraws hand

This movement should ultimately be performed rapidly and smoothly so that the hand is withdrawn in time to allow the toy to bounce back and forth.

Teacher behaviors

a) T demonstrates movement of toy by hitting it
b) T gives verbal cue, waits 5 seconds; if S responds correctly, T reinforces
c) T repeats verbal cue; if S responds correctly, T reinforces
d) T models behavior
e) T repeats verbal cue; if S responds correctly, T reinforces
f) T physically prompts by:
   1) placing slight pressure with one finger on S's elbow
   2) moving S's hand to toy

3) opening S's hand
4) pushing S's palm against toy
5) withdrawing S's hand
6) reinforcing

B. Nondominant hand

Follow the same sequence used with the dominant hand.

Pair primary and social reinforcement. As S's response becomes fairly consistent after teacher behavior b) or c), gradually reduce primary reinforcement to every third trial, but maintain social reinforcement. Difficulty may be encountered in S behavior 5. In this case, having someone behind S to immediately apply physical prompting to S's arm withdrawal after the hitting motion may be required to hasten mastery of this step.

Activity II Cue: "Splash the water." (Dominant and nondominant hand)

The student should be sitting or standing 10 inches behind a tray partially filled with lukewarm water.

Student behaviors	*Teacher behaviors*
1. S extends arm so that hand is directly over water	a) T demonstrates splashing the water
2. S opens hand	b) T continues as with Activity I
3. S slaps water with palm of hand	
4. S withdraws hand from water	After S learns to slap the water, the activity can develop into learning to splash the water in a purposeful direction away from S. Some object can be placed at the opposite end of the water tray and S taught to direct the the splash onto that object.
Slapping the water should be a quick motion, non-differentiating the movement of the hand into and out of the water.	
	Reinforce the same as with Activity I. Instructional setting should be varied to outdoors when possible, to art room, swimming pool, etc.

172

Activity III Cue: "Push the ball." (Dominant and nondominant hand)

This activity can be started by using a large balloon since it is lighter in weight and requires less muscle strength. As skill is developed, change to a large ball about 12 inches in diameter.

Student behaviors	*Teacher behaviors*
Same as for Activity I.	Same as for Activity I. It is helpful to have a third person involved to receive and return the ball. This also adds motivation as a game atmosphere evolves. Emphasis should not be placed at this time on catching the ball. *S* should be sitting, if physically possible, on the floor with legs extended and apart in front of him. Otherwise, place *S* at the end of a table so the ball can be rolled along the table top. *S* should not be permitted to pick up the ball and throw it, but should be reinforced only when pushing the ball on a supporting surface. The instructional setting should be varied to a gym, playground, etc. Reinforce according to Activity I. Gradually fade physical and verbal prompting as *S* learns to push the ball to the other person.

5. *Bilateral reach*

Objective: On making eye contact with an object 12 inches in front of him, the student will move both hands toward the object and grasp it in both hands.

Materials: cup or glass
large stuffed toy
large sheet of paper or aluminum foil

Activity I Cue: "Pick up the cup."

Student behaviors	Teacher behaviors
Same as Fine Motor I, Activity I, only using *both* hands.	Same as Fine Motor I, Activity I, using *S*'s two hands. Primary reinforcement can consist of liquid in the cup that *S* is helped to drink after picking up the cup. (junior cup with top is recommended.) This will reinforce the picking up behavior as well as initiate self-feeding.

Activity II Cue: "Pick up the paper."

Student behaviors	Teacher behaviors
Same as Fine Motor I, Activity I, only using *both* hands.	a) *T* demonstrates noise and light reflection (from aluminum foil) that occur when paper is picked up b) Follow Fine Motor I, Activity I, with *S* using both hands concurrently

Activity III Cue: "Pick up the _____."

A large stuffed toy is used in this activity. Procedures follow those for the previous two activities. This works especially well for those students who enjoy cuddling soft toys. Reinforcement can be several minutes of cuddling the toy picked up, and other primary reinforcers may not be necessary.

6. *Voluntary release*

Objective: With the object retained in the palmar grasp of one hand (or both hands), the student will release object so that hand contact is no longer maintained (with dominant and nondominant hands and bilaterally with large objects). Initially, release will be onto table top or floor or into *T*'s hand. Work into purposeful placement of released object, e.g., into container or specified spot on table.

Materials: ball at least 12 inches in diameter
bean bags
paper and wastebasket

Activity I Cue: "Drop the toy." (Dominant and nondominant hand)

Student behaviors	Teacher behaviors

1. *S* retains object in hand
2. *S* opens hand to release object
	a) *T* hands object to *S* or lets *S* reach for and pick up object
	b) *T* gives verbal cue, waits 5 seconds; if *S* responds correctly, *T* reinforces
	c) *T* repeats verbal cue; if *S* responds correctly, *T* reinforces
	d) *T* models behavior
	e) *T* repeats verbal cue; if *S* responds correctly, *T* reinforces
	f) *T* physically prompts by:
	  1) rubbing various surfaces of arm and hand
	  2) partially opening *S*'s fingers
	  3) completely opening *S*'s fingers
	  4) reinforcing
	  5) directing *S*'s attention to dropped object

Importance should be placed on directing *S*'s attention to the dropped object. She should be made keenly aware that the object is no longer in her hand and that her voluntary action caused this to be. Ways to thus direct her attention could include attaching a string to the object and tying the other end around *S*'s wrist. When the object is released and falls, *S* will be able to feel the weight, which will more readily draw her attention to the object. Reinforcement may be held in proximity to the dropped object to draw attention in that direction.

Activity II Cue: "Give me the toy." (Dominant and nondominant hand)

Student behaviors	Teacher behaviors
1. *S* retains object in hand 2. *S* extends hand to *T*'s	a) *T* holds hand out to *S* and gives verbal cue; if *S* responds correctly, *T* reinforces

175

3. *S* places object in *T*'s hand
4. *S* opens hand to release object
5. *S* withdraws hand

b) If correct response is not made, *T* places hand directly under object held by *S* and repeats cue; *T* reinforces if correct response is made

c) *T* physically prompts if necessary by gradually removing object from *S*'s hand; *T* reinforces

d) As *S* learns to release object, *T* should move her hand back gradually to 12 inches from *S*'s and require *S* to move arm to meet *T*'s hand. To teach *S* to withdraw hand, it might be necessary to have a third person to prompt from behind *S*

Activity III Cue: "Bounce the ball." (Bilateral release)

Student behaviors	*Teacher behaviors*
1. *S* holds ball in both hands (one on each side)	a) *T* demonstrates letting ball bounce
2. *S* extends arms away from body	b) *T* gives verbal cue; if *S* responds correctly, *T* reinforces
3. *S* abducts hands from ball simultaneously	c) *T* models
	d) *T* repeats verbal cue; if *S* responds correctly, *T* reinforces
	e) *T* physically prompts, then reinforces
	f) *T* directs attention to ball as in Activity I

The instructional setting should vary to outdoors with various colors, textures, and sizes of balls as learning progresses.

Activity IV Cue: "Drop the paper in the basket." (Dominant and nondominant hand)

176

Student behaviors	Teacher behaviors
1. *S* squeezes paper to crumple it	a) Basket should be immediately beside *S* to begin instruction; if *S* is mobile, basket can gradually be moved farther away so that *S* must move to basket before depositing paper
2. *S* holds paper in hand	
3. *S* moves to basket	
4. *S* extends hand over basket	
5. *S* releases paper so that it falls into basket	b) The act of voluntarily releasing the object should be mastered by *S* by this time. Purposeful placement should be the object of this activity, and reinforcement should follow only proper placement of the released object.
	c) Manual gestures should be initially used by *T* to show required placement while giving verbal cue; fade gestures

7. *Transfer from hand to hand*

Objective: *S* will move grasped object from one hand to the other (L–R and R–L) and hold object for more than 2 seconds.

Materials: small ball, block, or any suitable object than can be held in one hand

Activity I Cue: "Put it in the other hand."

Student behaviors	Teacher behaviors
1. *S* reaches for and picks up object with one hand	a) *T* demonstrates behavior
	b) *T* gives verbal cue to pick up object
2. *S* brings hands together in midline	c) *T* gives verbal cue to put it in the other hand
3. *S* opens free hand	d) *T* models behavior from point where *S*'s response breaks down and rewards steps in successive approximation to end behavior
4. *S* grasps object with free hand	
5. *S* releases object from first hand	
	e) *T* physically prompts

177

6. *S* maintains grasp with second hand for 2 seconds or more

   f) *T* has *S* transfer L–R and R–L

The task may need to be modified for students with one incapacitated arm or hand. Reaching for the object may be substituted for by *T* placing object in *S*'s nondominant hand and then requiring transfer. *S* may be unable to bring hands together in midline. Dominant hand will then need to reach across the body to grasp the object held in the nondominant hand.

Behavior can be strengthened by using all opportunities to teach. Example: Hand an eating utensil to *S* at mealtime and request him to put it in the other hand before beginning to eat.

Activity II Cue: "Pass the ball."

May be done with two teachers and student, or with one teacher and several students. The instructional setting is sitting on the floor or in chairs in a tight circle.

Student behaviors	*Teacher behaviors*
1. *S* grasps ball with left hand from person on his left	a) *T* may stand in center of circle and physically prompt each student through correct behavior
2. *S* brings ball to midline of body	
3. *S* transfers ball to right hand	b) As ball comes to each person, *T* calls his name before giving the verbal cue to direct his attention to ball
4. *S* extends right hand to person seated on his right	
	c) *T* gradually fades all prompts so that passing behavior becomes spontaneous
Reverse order so that *S* grasps with right hand and passes with left hand	d) *T* avoids the tendency to make irrelevant comments during activity
	e) Persistent throwing or dropping of ball should be ignored as much as possible by focusing on reinforcing appropriate passing

Primary reinforcers may be a hindrance in such a group activity and should be used only as necessary. Praise and *T* attention should be relied on heavily, and the natural reinforcement of the game should be enough to maintain behavior.

8. *Scissors grasp*

Objective: The student will grasp object with partial opposition of thumb to one or two fingers on the thumb side of the hand.

Materials: jumbo crayon and drawing paper
pull or talking toy with pull-string

Activity I Cue: "Pick up the crayon."

Student behaviors	*Teacher behaviors*
1. S picks up crayon and grips 2. S picks up crayon with point of crayon on little finger end and turns palm toward body 3. S picks up crayon about 1 to 2 inches from point with tips of fingers (thumb on one side and fingers on other side of crayon) and palm turned toward body 4. S picks up crayon about 1 to 2 inches from point with thumb, with first and middle fingers and palm turned toward body	S may tend to revert to palmar grasp in holding a crayon. Make sure the crayon is jumbo size and place S's fingers in proper position. T may need to place one or two of his fingers between crayon and S's palm to condition S to hold crayon away from palm. Modeling may be of limited value, since S will need to feel the correct position of fingers. Physical prompting and manipulation are important. Reinforce each step and use successive approximation to proper grasp as outlined in S behaviors.

Activity II Cue: "Pull the string."

Student behaviors	*Teacher behaviors*
1. S reaches for ring on end of string 2. S grasps ring between thumb and one or two fingers on thumb side of hand with palm facing down or toward body	a) T demonstrates action of toy by pulling string b) T tells S to pick up ring (ring should be large and painted a bright color initially; gradually fade these prompts)

179

3. *S* maintains grasp
while pulling ring

c) *T* physically manipulates
proper grasp
d) *T* gives verbal cue to pull
string; if *S* responds correctly, *T* reinforces
e) *T* may need to hold *S*'s
fingers in place several times
while leading him through
the pulling motion; *T* reinforces each time
f) Major emphasis should be
placed on proper grasp, not
on the ability to pull the
string
g) Primary reinforcement
should be faded as pulling is
mastered. Reinforcement of
the toy's action should be
sufficient at this point,
paired with social reinforcement from *T*.
h) Instructional setting should
vary to outdoors for pull-
toys and other appropriate
materials

For better functioning children, using scissors is a good activity
to further develop this basic grasp.

9. *Pincer grasp*

Objective: The student will pick up object with tip of thumb and
tip of index finger (and/or middle finger) and maintain
pincer grasp for 10 seconds, with dominant and nondominant hand.

Materials: tennis ball, small box, eraser, or other objects of com-
parable size, pencil, paper clip, buttons, or other small
objects, medicine dropper, water and container

Activity I Cue: "Pick up the _____."

A. Large item

Student behaviors	*Teacher behaviors*
1. *S* reaches for object	Same as for Fine Motor VIII,
2. *S* touches object with fingers	Activity I

180

3. *S* picks up object using all fingers
4. *S* holds object with fingertips
5. *S* maintains grasp for:
       2 seconds
       4 seconds
       6 seconds
       10 seconds

B. Small item

Student behaviors	*Teacher behaviors*
1. *S* reaches for object	Same as above
2. *S* touches object with fingers	
3. *S* picks up object using thumb and tip of index finger (and/or middle finger)	
4. *S* holds object in pincer grasp	
5. *S* maintains pincer grasp for: 2 seconds 4 seconds 6 seconds 10 seconds	

Activity II (using medicine dropper and water play) Cue: "Do this."

Student behaviors	*Teacher behaviors*
1. *S* picks up medicine dropper	a) *T* gives verbal cue and demonstrates
2. *S* holds dropper by bulb end between thumb and tip of index finger (and/or middle finger)	b) *T* repeats verbal cue; if *S* responds correctly, *T* reinforces
	c) *T* models and repeats verbal cue; if *S* responds correctly, *T* reinforces
3. *S* puts tip of dropper in water	d) *T* physically prompts by:
4. *S* pinches bulb of dropper	1) taking *S*'s hand that is holding medicine dropper and putting tip of dropper in the water

181

5. *S* lifts tip of dropper out of water
6. *S* pinches bulb of dropper

2) squeezing *S*'s fingers to draw up water; reinforcing
3) moving *S*'s hand so dropper comes out of water
4) squeezing *S*'s fingers so water is released from dropper, reinforcing
5) adding food coloring to water to help keep *S*'s attention

Other suggested activities:

a) picking up small bits of food
b) zipping up coat
c) using light switch
d) playing finger cymbals

10. *Manipulating small objects with purpose*

A. Picking up buttons, putting in slot

Objective: Using a pincer grasp, student will pick up 5 buttons, one at a time, and put them through slot.

Materials: buttons, different sizes (5 of each size)
buttonhole board, shoe box with slot in lid, or coffee can with slot in top

Student behaviors

1. *S* picks up 1-1/2 inch button
2. *S* holds it in pincer grasp
3. *S* locates slot
4. *S* puts button 1/3 way through
5. *S* puts button 1/2 way through
6. *S* puts button 3/4 way through
7. *S* releases button from grasp

Teacher behaviors

a) *T* demonstrates
b) *T* gives instruction "Put the button in the hole;" if *S* responds correctly, *T* reinforces
c) *T* models behavior
d) *T* repeats verbal cue; if *S* responds correctly, *T* reinforces
e) *T* verbally prompts; if *S* approximates behavior but has button turned crosswise to slot, say "Turn it around" or "Try another way."

8. S pushes button completely through slot using tips of thumb, index, and/or middle finger

Follow above sequence using buttons
1 inch in diameter
3/4 inch in diameter
1/2 inch in diameter

f) T physically prompts and reinforces
g) Slot or button hole should be blatantly outlined in a bright color, then faded
h) T pairs primary and social reinforcement and fades primary

B. Stringing beads

Objective: Given lace and beads, the student will string 5 beads.

Materials: lace
beads, varying size from 1 inch downward (5 of each size)

Student behaviors

1. S pulls end of lace
2. S holds bead with one hand and pulls lace
3. S holds bead, pushes lace final 1/2 of the way through bead and pulls lace
4. S holds bead, pushes lace final 3/4 of way through bead and pulls lace
5. S holds bead, inserts lace into hole and pushes through bead to end of lace
6. S picks up bead in one hand and point end of lace in other hand; inserts lace into hole and pushes through bead to end of lace
7. S strings 2 beads
8. S strings 3 beads
9. S strings 4 beads
10. S strings 5 beads

Teacher behaviors

a) T knots one end of lace so beads cannot fall off
b) Other end of lace should be maintained in a point by means of dried glue, etc. This end should initially be painted a bright color, then faded.
c) T holds bead and lace and pushes lace through bead until end is through far enough to be easily grasped
d) T instructs S to pull end of lace; if S responds correctly, T reinforces
e) T physically prompts if necessary; reinforces
f) T hands bead to S; T pushes lace through bead and instructs S to pull lace with free hand; T prompts and reinforces as above
g) T gives S a bead and the point end of lace to hold, then instructs S to push the lace through the bead

Repeat with smaller beads.

h) *T* completes pushing lace through bead when *S* has pushed it through 1/2 way

i) *T* instructs *S* to pull end of lace; *T* prompts and reinforces as above

j) Follow *T* behaviors g), h), and i) with *S* pushing 3/4 of way and completely through, then to end of lace without assistance

k) *T* lays lace and bead on table in front of *S* and instructs *S* to string the beads

C. Unscrewing top

Objective: Given a container with a top screwed on, the student will unscrew top and remove it from the container.

Materials: nonbreakable container with screw top at least 6 inches in diameter

nonbreakable container with screw top that fits into *S*'s hand

nonbreakable container, such as toothpaste tube, which requires use of fingers to unscrew

reinforcer to be placed inside container

Large container with a 6-inch or larger top

Student behaviors	Teacher behaviors
1. *S* secures container between knees	a) *T* codes lid by using colored paint or magic marker. Set lid on container but do not screw. Paint a line that extends from just on top of lid to about 2 inches down container. A see-through container would be preferable
2. *S* grasps lid with palms, one hand on each side	
3. *S* twists lid to right (counterclockwise)	
4. *S* lifts lid off	
5. *S* places lid on floor or table beside container	b) *T* shows reinforcer to child and places the reinforcer in container
	c) *T* screws lid to closed position, but not tight

d) *T* can hold container so that
paint mark on container
(not lid) is facing *S*
e) *T* physically leads *S* through
behavior several times, using
the reinforcer in the container at the completion of the
behavior
f) Lining up the paint marks
can be a visual and verbal
cue for students capable of
matching
g) *T* fades physical prompts
h) When *S* has learned to unscrew top when *T* holds container, *T* puts container
between *S*'s knees and
teaches behavior from this
origin

Container with lid that fits into *S*'s hand

Student behaviors	*Teacher behaviors*
1. *S* holds container with nondominant hand	a) *T* codes as above
2. *S* grasps lid with dominant hand	b) *T* uses reinforcer as above
3. *S* twists lid to R in counterclockwise direction	c) *T* teaches as above, except to have *S* hold container with one hand and unscrew lid with the other hand. Should start out on table top, on floor, in lap, and then with no supporting surface if possible
4. *S* lifts lid off	
5. *S* places lid on table beside container	

Toothpaste tube

Student behaviors	*Teacher behaviors*
1. *S* holds tube with nondominant hand	Same as above
2. *S* grasps top with fingers of dominant hand	
3. *S* twists top to right (counterclockwise)	

4. *S* lifts top off
5. *S* places top on table

D. Turns doorknob (opens and closes door)

Objective: The student stands to side of door, grasps and turns knob, pulls door open, then closes door

Door should be lightweight and swing freely.

Student behaviors	*Teacher behaviors*
1. *S* grasps doorknob and closes final 1/4 of way	a) *T* gives verbal cue "Close the door," models behavior and physically prompts, and reinforces
2. *S* grasps doorknob and closes 1/2 of way	
3. *S* grasps doorknob and closes 3/4 of way	b) Same as a
4. *S* grasps doorknob and closes door	c) Same as a
	d) Same as a
5. *S* stands to side of door, grasps doorknob and turns knob	e) *T* gives verbal cue "Open the door," shows model behavior of turning knob, and physically prompts. *S* may need to use both hands at first. *T* reinforces
6. *S* stands to side of door, turns knob and pulls toward self	
7. *S* stands to side of door and opens 1/4 of way	f) Same as e
	g) Same as e
	h) Same as e
	i) Same as e
8. *S* stands to side of door, grasps knob, turns knob, and pulls door open 1/2 of way	j) *T* gives verbal cue "Open the door," waits for *S* to complete behavior, then gives verbal cue "Close the door." *T* models, prompts, and reinforces as above
9. *S* stands to side of door, grasps knob, turns knob, and pulls door open 3/4 of way	
10. *S* stands to side of door, grasps and turns knob, pulls door open, then closes door	

E. Picture puzzle (requires discrimination)

Objective: Given a picture puzzle, student will take all pieces out of form and put all pieces back in random order. (The number of steps depends on the number of pieces in the puzzle chosen.)

Student behaviors	Teacher behaviors
1. S removes 1 puzzle piece	a) T gives verbal cue "Take this piece out" and indicates one piece. T models, physically prompts, and reinforces
2. S replaces same piece	
3. S removes 2 puzzle pieces	b) T gives verbal cue "Put this piece in the puzzle." T indicates piece to be replaced and places in form where it fits. T verbally prompts by using phrases such as "Turn it around," "Try another way." T physically prompts and reinforces
4. S replaces these 2 pieces	
5. S removes 3 puzzle pieces	
6. S replaces 3 pieces	
	c) T gives verbal cue "Take these pieces out" and indicates pieces. T models, physically prompts, reinforces
	d) Same as b
	e) Same as c
	f) Same as b
	g) T fades prompting and increases the number of pieces in puzzles

F. Multiple shape box (requires discrimination)

Objective: Given a shape box and blocks of 5 different shapes, the student will put all shapes in the proper slots in the shape box.

Student behaviors	Teacher behaviors
1. S puts 1 shape in corresponding hole (only one hole showing)	a) T places shape on table in front of S and gives verbal cue "Put it in the box." T models, prompts, and reinforces
2. S puts 1 shape in corresponding hole (2 holes showing)	
3. S puts 2 shapes in corresponding holes (2 holes showing)	b) Same as a. T rotates box so holes are in different positions
4. S puts 2 shapes in corresponding holes (3 holes showing)	c) T repeats these behaviors for the remaining shapes

5. S puts 3 shapes in corresponding holes (4
   holes showing)
6. S puts 4 shapes in corresponding holes (4
   holes showing)
7. S puts 4 shapes in corresponding holes (5
   holes showing)
8. S puts 5 shapes in corresponding holes (5
   holes showing)

This program was developed by Phyllis Brocklehurst under my supervision. It has been successfully used with a number of profoundly handicapped children.

INSTRUCTIONAL GUIDELINES

This brief review of research on motor skill training with the severely and profoundly handicapped has revealed two basic orientations. The sensory-motor training theory, espoused by Kephart of Doman-Delacato, has had limited success in accelerating motor development. On the other hand, a behavior modification training approach stressing the critical role of stimulus support, reinforcement contingencies, and multiple environmental stimulation, has been effective.

For the following reasons, behavioral training methods are strongly recommended to teachers who attempt to increase gross and fine-motor skills in children with severe handicaps:

1. Many severely involved children with physical disability do not actively respond to passive stimulation or presentation of different novel stimuli. Physical prompting (Auxter, 1971) and demonstration of target skills by the teacher are required to elicit movement from the child. This may be one reason why the patterning method

advocated by Doman and Delacato had some success with the retarded (Neman et al., 1975).

2. Reinforcement is necessary to increase and maintain the motivation of severely and profoundly handicapped children (Campbell, 1974). Motor activity may be hard work, and incentives must be offered if gains are to be made. Reinforcement should be contingent on approximations of the target motor skill being taught.

3. Motor activities and tasks must be sufficiently novel. Without a variety of learning materials, training sessions will become tedious and boring.

4. Motor skills must be presented in small behavioral increments to ensure frequent success. Furthermore, the progress made in the program can serve as reinforcing feedback to the teacher and parents.

5. The child must be positioned so that he/she can be easily reached. For some children, this is best done from behind, but it is usually best to sit facing the child at his level.

6. The following instructional model for training fine motor tasks should be used.

   A. Give the appropriate verbal cue.
   B. If there is no response, model the task.
   C. If there is still no response, physically guide the child through the target behavior.
   D. Use backward chaining so that the child completes the task from the point at which he or she is able to do so independently.

7. Use a multisensory approach to tasks on which a child is having difficulty by having him or her look at the task, then physically help the child move a finger around the material you are working with as you identify the object verbally.

8. Make certain that the child is attending to the task before giving instructions.
9. In planning fine motor objectives, plan a time period in which you expect to see some success or improvement. If there is no improvement by that time, consider changing materials or breaking the task down into smaller steps.
10. Be sure the child is properly positioned for good body alignment and optimal visual range and movements.
11. Help the child become physically relaxed before beginning a training sequence. Stainback and Stainback (1976) recommend the following methods to promote relaxation in stiff children:

    A. Keep the environment free of distracting stimuli.
    B. Talk calmly to the child.
    C. Try gentle rocking in the fetal position.
    D. Hydrotherapy, i.e., placing child in warm circulating water, may also be helpful.

12. Adapted chairs should be prescribed by qualified professionals. They may be introduced to the child in 15- to 30-minute daily intervals, which can be gradually extended from 3 to 6 hours.
13. In reviewing all programs, it appears that the behavior modification approach is more efficient. Training time with behavior modification was significantly shorter in most cases than with sensory-motor training.

SUMMARY

Much published material is available in the area of perceptual-motor skill development and adaptive physical education (e.g., Cratty, 1969; Daniels & Davies, 1975), and the interested reader is encouraged to consult this work. The purpose of this chapter was to familiarize those teaching the severely and profoundly handicapped with methods and techniques that can facilitate gross and fine motor development. An effort was made to identify literature in the area of motor skills that was directly related to the learning and behavior characteristics of severely handicapped persons.

REFERENCES

Auxter, D. Motor skill development in the profoundly retarded. *Training School Bulletin,* 1971, *60,* 5–9.

Bobath, B. Motor development: Its effects on general development and application to the treatment of cerebral palsy. *Physiotherapy,* 1971, *49,* 1279–1288.

Bradley, W., Konicki, G., & Leedy, C. *Daily sensorimotor training activities.* New York: Educational Activities, Inc., 1968.

Bricker, D. D., Davis, J., Wahlin, L., & Evans, J. *A motor training program for the developmentally young.* Miami, Florida: University of Miami, 1976.

Brown, L., Scheuerman, N., & Crowner, T. *Madison's alternative to zero exclusion: Toward an integrated therapy model for teaching motor, tracking, and scanning skills to severely handicapped students.* Madison Public Schools: Madison, Wisconsin, 1976.

Campbell, J. Physical fitness and the MR: A review of research. *Mental Retardation,* 1974, *11,* 26–29.

Chandler, L., & Adams, M. Multiply handicapped children motivated for ambulation through behavior modification. *Physical Therapy,* 1972, *52,* 339–401.

Cratty, B. J. *Motor activity and the education of retardates.* Philadelphia: Lea & Febiger, 1969.

Daniels, J., & Davies, E. *Adaptive physical education.* New York: Harper & Row, 1975.

Edgar, C. L. Effects of sensory motor training on adaptive behavior. *American Journal of Mental Deficiency,* 1969, *73,* 713–719.

Frostig, M. Visual perception, integrative functions, and academic learning. *Journal of Learning Disabilities,* 1972, *5,* 15.

Fuller, P. P. Operant conditioning of a vegetative human organism. *American Journal of Psychology,* 1949, *62,* 587–599.

Goshgarian, N. K. Visual preferences in retarded infants. Unpublished master's thesis, University of Wisconsin, 1968.

Grove, D., & Walker, B. Contingent feedback for training children to propel their wheelchairs. *Physical Therapy,* 1976, *56(7),* 815–820.

Horner, R. D. Establishing use of crutches by a mentally retarded spina bifida child. *Journal of Applied Behavior Analysis,* 1971, *4(3),* 183–190.

Kephart, N. C. *The slow learner in the classroom.* Columbus, Ohio: Charles Merrill, Inc., 1960.

Landesmann-Dwyer, S. A description and modification of the behavior of nonambulatory profoundly mentally retarded children. Unpublished doctoral dissertation, University of Washington, 1974.

Landesmann-Dwyer, S., & Sackett, G. A research strategy for studying nonambulatory profoundly mentally retarded individuals. In C. Cleland & L. Talkington (Eds.), *Research with profoundly retarded: A conference proceedings.* Austin, Texas: University of Texas Press, 1975.

Lederman, S. J. Behavioral and heart rate responses to visual stimuli in profoundly retarded children. Unpublished master's thesis, University of Wisconsin, 1969.

LeWinn, E., Doman, G., Delacato, C., Doman, R., Spitz, E., & Thomas, E. Neurological organization: The basis for learning. In J. Hellmuth (Ed.), *Learning Disorders* (Vol. 2). Seattle: Child Publications, Inc., 1966.

Loynd, J., & Barclay, A. A case study in developing ambulation in a profoundly retarded child. *Behavior Research and Therapy,* 1970, *8,* 270.

Macauley, M., & MacMillan, M. Teaching severely retarded children to walk. *Developmental Medicine and Child Neurology,* 1970, *1,* 549–556.

Neman, R., Roos, P., McCann, B., Menolascino, F., & Heal, L. An experimental evaluation of sensorimotor patterning used with mentally retarded children. *American Journal of Mental Deficiency,* 1975, *79,* 372–384.

Piaget, J. *Play, dreams, and imitation in childhood.* New York: W. W. Norton, 1951.

Piper, T. J., & Mackinnon, R. C. Operant conditioning of a profoundly retarded individual reinforced via a stomach fistula. *American Journal of Mental Deficiency,* 1969, *73(4),* 627–630.

Rice, H., & McDaniel, M. Operant behavior in vegetative patients. *Psychological Record,* 1966, *16,* 279–281.

Rice, H., McDaniel, M., Stallings, V., & Gatz, G. Operant behavior in vegetative patients: II. *Psychological Record,* 1967, *17,* 449–460.

Stainback, S., & Stainback, W. Teaching the profoundly handicapped in the public school setting: Some considerations. *AAESPH Review,* 1976, *1(3),* 1–17.

Utley, B., Holvoet, J., & Barnes, K. Handling, positioning, and feeding the physically handicapped. In *Educational Programming for the Severely and Profoundly Handicapped.* Reston, Virginia: CEC Publications, 1977.

Webb, R. Sensory motor training of the profoundly retarded. *American Journal of Mental Deficiency,* 1969, *69,* 283–294.

Wilson, V., & Parks, S. R. Promoting ambulation in the severely retarded child. *Mental Retardation,* 1970, *8,* 17–19.

Zigler, E., & Seitz, V. On "an experimental evaluation of sensorimotor patterning:" a critique. *American Journal of Mental Deficiency,* 1975, *79,* 483–492.

Chapter 6

LANGUAGE

Development of language skills in the severely handicapped has received increased attention in recent years (Garcia & DeHaven, 1974; Hollis & Carrier, 1975; Lloyd, 1976; Snyder, Lovitt, & Smith, 1975). Many severely and profoundly handicapped individuals are nonverbal and display primitive forms of communication. These communication deficits are often compounded by the limited language directed toward the severely handicapped. Parents and teachers, after repeated failures at eliciting speech, eventually minimize the number of verbal instructions and conversation and rely only on demonstration and physical guidance.

This chapter reviews research in receptive and expressive language and discusses alternate modes of communication for severely and profoundly handicapped students. Selected instructional language programs in relevant content areas are presented, along with guidelines for implementing a language program.

RECEPTIVE LANGUAGE

INSTRUCTION FOLLOWING.   One major area of receptive language that has been researched is instruction following (Brown, Bellamy, Tang, & Klemme, 1971; Craighead, O'-Leary, & Allen, 1973; Streifel & Weatherby, 1976; Waldron, 1975; Wehman, Schutz, Renzaglia, & Karan, 1977; Whitman, Zakaras, & Chardos, 1971). This is an important program area of language training because noncompliance may interfere with the development of appropriate social skills and progress in the classroom.

The typical training procedures involved in training students to follow instructions has been identifying several instructions or commands and reinforcing compliance with these instructions. In a study by Whitman and his associates (1971), generalization to a different set of untrained instructions was accomplished once an initial set of instructions had been taught. Using a related procedure with a profoundly handicapped "autistic" child, Craighead et al. (1973) trained instruction following and programmed transfer of training across adults and peers. However, generalization was not achieved in another study which used similar training procedures with profoundly handicapped children (Streifel & Weatherby, 1976).

Wehman et al. (1977) increased compliance with instructions in a profoundly handicapped workshop client. A positive practice procedure was used across four target instructions. Every time the trainee did not comply, he was manually guided very rapidly through the instruction 20 times. He also received positive social reinforcement if he complied. The response was generalized across all the commands after the first command was taught.

Effective training of instruction following requires a transfer of stimulus control from the teacher's verbal cues to instructions from different trainers and across environments. Studies are needed in which two- and three-step instructions are trained. Acquisition of multiple instruction following across different settings has not been documented with severely and profoundly handicapped students. Classroom teachers and speech therapists who develop receptive language programs that emphasize instruction following must expand the range of training environments.

Table 6–1 presents a sample program to illustrate how instruction following can be taught to noncompliant students and how transfer across environments and persons can be programmed. This program was implemented with primary age, trainable retarded children.

NOUN COMPREHENSION. The ability to discriminate different objects is a fundamental level of language development critical to most aspects of verbal communication. Furthermore, to use communication (picture) boards, Bliss symbols, or other manual types of language, it will be necessary to respond correctly to a cue such as "Point to the ball" or "Show me the food." Acquisition of this level of language will facilitate production (expression) of language.

EXPRESSIVE LANGUAGE

Language programs that emphasize the production of speech and language have been developed by utilizing modeling and shaping procedures (Garcia, Guess, & Byrnes, 1973; Guess, Sailor, Rutherford, & Baer, 1968). Development of vocal imitation as a prerequisite to more advanced language has also been documented (Garcia, Baer, & Firestone, 1971; Schroeder & Baer, 1972; Sloane, Johnson, & Harris, 1968). In the study by Sloane et al., mouth and tongue imitations were included among motor responses. Vocal training consisted of modeling a combi-

Table 6-1. Instruction Following Program

Baseline Procedures

Objectives: In the environments A, B, or C, with teachers A, B, or C, when given the specific instruction, the child will carry it out 90 percent of the time for three consecutive days.

Environment A: Children's regular classroom. The time will be in the afternoon while the children are working on individual needs and resting. The teacher will be seated at the desk facing children. Children are seated at two semicircular tables. The teacher's desk is about 5 to 8 feet from the children's tables.

Teacher A: The teacher gives following instructions: Sit down, stand up, bring me the pencil, and raise your hand.

Note: No reinforcement is given during baseline.

General Procedure: When the teacher is seated at the desk, she will say the student's name and the command:

1. "Jonathan, *come to me.*" The student must get up and walk directly to the teacher within 10 seconds. For a correct response, the teacher will mark plus; for an incorrect response or no response, the teacher will mark minus.
2. "Jonathan, *sit down.*" The student must walk to his own seat and sit down within 10 seconds.
3. "Jonathan, *bring me the pencil.*" The student must walk straight to the teacher and hand the pencil to her within 10 seconds.
4. "Jonathan, *raise your hand.*" The student must raise only one arm above his head within 10 seconds.
5. "Jonathan, *stand up.*" The student must stand up and remain standing next to his chair; he must not walk away from it. He must comply within 10 seconds.

This same procedure will be followed in the cafeteria and in the occupational room. The teacher will *not* reprimand or praise the child. She simply says "thank you" after each instruction.

The instructions will be given four times each during a specific session. They will be in a mixed order so that the children will not know exactly which direction will be given at a certain time. During each session, there will be 20 trials that the child will be expected to follow (five trials of each command).

Baseline Environment B (Objective same as A): School cafeteria; children are seated around the lunch table. There are nine children and three adults. Children will be finishing lunch and throwing away their trays.

General Procedure: The same as in Environment A, except that the person giving the instructions must speak much louder because the cafeteria is noisier than the regular classroom.

Baseline Environment C (Objective same as Environments A and B): Classroom where children go for occupational therapy. Children are all seated around a table. Four adults are with the children at the table (two teachers and two aides). The teacher giving the instructions is separated from the children. She is seated at the teacher's desk, about 6 feet from the large table.

General Procedure: Same as for Environments A and B.

Instructional Procedures

1. *Sit Down*

Objective: Given the command "sit down," the child will comply 90 percent of the time for 3 consecutive days.

General Procedure: Teacher A, B, or C says to S: "Michael, *sit down*." Be sure to use the child's name. If he does so within 10 seconds, she gives verbal praise: "Good boy, Michael. You are sitting down just the way I told you to!"

If the student does not comply within 10 seconds, the command is repeated. If the student does so he is given verbal praise and a hug. If the student does not comply, the teacher points to the chair and says "Michael, sit down in that chair."

If the student still does not comply, the teacher will physically lead the child to the chair and say, "I want you to sit down in this chair." After helping the child to his seat, the teacher will say, "That is what I want you to do when I tell you to sit down."

This procedure is to be followed until the child will obey all three teachers in all three environments. (The procedure may have to be altered somewhat to fit the specific needs of the children.)

2. *Stand Up*

Objective: Given the instruction "stand up," the student will stand up by his chair and not walk over to the teacher or to anywhere else 90 percent of the time for 3 consecutive days.

General Procedure: Teacher A, B, or C will say to the student: "Michael, stand up." If child stands up within 10 seconds, the teacher will give verbal praise to the child. "That's really great that you stood up," or "I'm so happy you listened to me." If the child does not stand up, the teacher will repeat the verbal command: "Michael, stand up." If he does so, the teacher hugs him or gives some type of physical reinforcement.

If he still does not comply, then the teacher will say, "Michael, I am standing up" (she stands up) and then she says, "Okay Michael, now you stand up." If he does so, he gets a pat on the back and verbal praise. If he still does not comply with the verbal command, the teacher takes the child and physically stands him up saying, "This is what I want you to do when I tell you to stand up."

3. *Come to Me*

Objective: Given the instruction "Come to me," the child will stop what he is doing and walk to the teacher within 10 seconds 90 percent of the time for 3 consecutive days.

General Procedure: The teacher says to the student: "Michael, come to me." If the child complies within 10 seconds, the teacher gives him verbal praise. ("Very good, Michael, you came right to me when I called you!") If the child does not come to the teacher, she repeats the command "Come to me." If he does, the teacher pats him on the back and also gives verbal praise. If he does not, the teacher walks to the child and takes him by the hand. She leads him back to her original seat at the desk and says, "Michael, when I tell you to come to me, I want you to walk right over to me." She leads him back to his seat and returns to hers. She says, "Michael, come to me." If he does, he gets a big hug and a fuss made over him. Continue this procedure until child complies with criteria.

4. *Raise Your Hand*

Objective: When given the verbal instruction "Raise your hand," the child will do so within 10 seconds 90 percent of the time for 3 consecutive days.

General Procedure: The teacher says to the student, "Michael, raise your hand." If he complies, the teacher will give verbal praise. If he does not comply, the teacher repeats the verbal command, "Raise your hand, Michael." If he does so, the teacher says "Good, Michael. I am really pleased with you," along with physical reinforcement. If the student does not comply, the teacher will raise her hand and say, "Michael, I am raising my hand. Now you raise your hand." If he does so the teacher gives verbal and physical praise. If the student fails to comply, the teacher will go over to the child and physically raise his hand and say, "This is what I want you to do when I tell you to raise your hand."

5. *Bring Me the Pencil*

Objective: Given the pencil and the verbal cue, "Bring me the pencil," the child will walk straight to the teacher and hand her the pencil. The child will do this 90 percent of the time for 3 consecutive days.

General Procedure: The teacher or another student in the room gives the child a pencil. Let some time elapse before giving the verbal command, "Michael, bring me the pencil." If the child brings the pencil to the teacher, the teacher takes the pencil and gives child verbal praise. If the student does not comply, the teacher repeats command, "Michael, bring me the pencil." If the child complies, the teacher takes the pencil and gives the child verbal praise. If the student still does not comply, the teacher goes to the child, puts the pencil in his hand, leads him to the teacher's desk, and says, "When I say to bring me the pencil, this is what I want you to do." At the desk, the teacher takes the pencil. Continue until the child follows the command.

This program was developed and implemented by Jeannie Donovan with a classroom of trainable level retarded children under my supervision.

nation of the previously learned mouth-tongue movements with verbal sounds.

Before acquiring motor and verbal imitation skills, severely handicapped students may have to be taught to sit appropriately and make eye contact with the teacher. Without eye contact and proper sitting, it is impossible to train the child how to imitate and how to learn the functional use of objects and other more advanced language skills. Table 6–2 details a teaching procedure for establishing eye contact, while Tables 6–3 and 6–4 list similar teaching procedures for developing motor and verbal imitation.

In teaching imitation skills and other rudimentary language, the teacher must be aware of the many variables that can influence the learning situation (e.g., Streifel, 1974). The following list includes some of the variables that may affect whether a teacher *(T)* will be able to help the student *(S)* acquire the skill, and also how *quickly* it will be acquired:

1. Are *T* and *S* face to face?
2. Does *T* get eye contact first?
3. Is *T* modeling the behavior when the child is attending?
4. Is *T* using the verbal cue, "Joan, do this."?

Table 6–2. Establishing Eye Contact

Behavioral Objective: The student (*S*) will turn to the teacher (*T*) when *T* calls his name and will maintain eye contact for 5 seconds four out of five times for 3 consecutive days.

Training Procedure:

1. *S* looks at *T* when *T* says *S*'s name.

   T says *S*'s name. Reinforce socially and with food if *S* looks at *T*. If not, after 5 seconds, either physically move his head or slowly move some food from in front of his eyes to yours. Deliver reinforcer as soon as *S* makes eye contact. Continue until *S* responds 8 out of 10 times when his name is called.

2. *S* maintains eye contact for 1 second.

   T says *S*'s name. Reinforce socially and with food 1 second after eye contact is made.

3. *S* maintains eye contact for 2 seconds.

   T says *S*'s name and reinforces only after eye contact is maintained for 2 seconds. Continue this procedure until *S* maintains eye contact for 5 seconds for 8 out of 10 trials. *T* builds from 1 to 5 seconds adding 1 second at each step.

4. *S* maintains eye contact without continuous reinforcement.

   T gradually withdraws reinforcers by reinforcing every second trial, then every third trial, then every fourth, then every fifth.

---

5. Is *T* providing physical prompting?
6. Is *T* allowing 5 seconds for the target response?
7. Is *T* reinforcing socially and/or with edibles? Is praise given expressively?
8. Is *T* recording data at the end of the session?
9. Does *T* reinforce *approximations* of the correct behavior?
10. Is *T* consistent with language cues, and not excessive in using different commands?
11. Does *T* remember to praise other children in the group who are sitting quietly?

Table 6–3. Training Motor Imitation
With Five Sample Motor Responses

Sit face to face with the child and make certain that you have gained eye contact. Use appropriate reinforcers.

Objective: The child will imitate the *modeled* behavior when given the verbal cue, "Michael, do this."

Steps to fading physical prompts for *raising arms*:

1. T moves S's arms to terminal position and holds them there.
2. T moves S's arms to terminal position and releases them.
3. T moves S's arms three-fourths of the way to terminal position and releases them.
4. T moves S's arms halfway to terminal position and releases them.
5. T starts moving S's arms upward and releases them.
6. T organizes S's hands with palms open, fingers spread, and releases them.
7. T touches S's hands.
8. T reaches toward S's hands.
9. T models behavior.

Steps to fading physical prompts for *ringing a bell*:

1. T moves S's hand with bell 10 times.
2. T moves S's hand with bell 8 times.
3. T moves S's hand with bell 5 times.
4. T moves S's hand with bell 2 times.
5. T organizes S's fingers around bell and lifts and releases it.
6. T organizes S's fingers around bell.
7. T moves S's hand toward bell and releases it.
8. T touches S's hand.
9. T reaches toward S's hand.
10. T models behavior.

Steps to fading physical prompts for *clapping hands*:

1. T moves S's hands to terminal position and continues with terminal behavior.
2. T moves S's hands together and releases them.
3. T moves S's hands three-fourths of the way together and releases them.
4. T moves S's hands toward each other and releases them.
5. T moves S's hands toward each other and releases them.
6. T touches S's hands.
7. T reaches toward S's hands.
8. T models behavior.

Steps to fading physical prompts for *drinking from a cup*:

1. *T* moves *S*'s hand with cup to mouth in proper drinking position and holds it there.
2. *T* moves *S*'s hand with cup to mouth in proper drinking position, with cup tilted, and releases hand.
3. *T* moves *S*'s hand with cup three-fourths of the way to mouth and releases hand.
4. *T* moves *S*'s hand with cup halfway to mouth and releases hand.
5. *T* starts to move *S*'s hand with cup and releases hand.
6. *T* organizes *S*'s hand around cup and releases hand.
7. *T* moves *S*'s hand toward cup and releases hand.
8. *T* touches *S*'s hand.
9. *T* reaches toward *S*'s hand.
10. *T* models behavior.

Steps to fading physical prompts for *touching head*:

1. *T* moves *S*'s hand to terminal position and holds it there.
2. *T* moves *S*'s hand to terminal position and releases it.
3. *T* moves *S*'s hand three-fourths of the way to head and releases it.
4. *T* starts to move *S*'s hand and releases it.
5. *T* organizes *S*'s hand in open-palm position.
6. *T* touches *S*'s hand.
7. *T* reaches toward *S*'s hand.
8. *T* models behavior.

Table 6–4. Verbal Imitation of Sounds and Words

Behavioral Objective: Given the verbal cue, "Say _____," the child will imitate _____ 8 out of 10 times during each session for 3 consecutive days.

Training Procedure:

1. *T* and *S* sit facing a mirror.
2. *T* asks *S* to make some sound he can produce.
3. *T* reinforces a correct sound production or a close approximation.
4. If *S* does not respond correctly, the sound is repeated for another trial.
5. If *S* does not respond correctly with a second trial, *T* holds *S*'s head close to his or hers and again says, "Say _____," while both look in the mirror.
6. If *S* does not respond at all, he should be ignored momentarily and another student should be given a trial.

---

12. Does *T* move from child to child so that no one child has to sit and wait for a long time?
13. Does *T* divide the classroom into small groups by the best physical arrangement of dividers and bookcases?
14. Does *T* situate herself close to children who have poor attending skills?
15. Does *T* allow enough trials and training sessions for skills to be acquired?

Bry and Nawas (1972) found that reinforcement was a necessary condition for training motor imitation to nonverbal and nonimitative retarded children. In their study it took over 3000 trials, 7 days a week at 45 minutes per session, before generalized imitative responses were developed. For teachers who find that motor imitation does not come quickly in their students, greater amounts of training and practice may be one solution to the problem.

Once imitation skills are acquired, the student can be taught the functional use of objects in the environment. This is the initial training phase in the excellent language program developed by Bricker, Ruder, and Vincent (1976). In the phase devoted to the functional use of objects, the student is asked to demonstrate the purpose of different objects in the environment. Table 6–5 displays the teaching procedures for developing the functional use of objects in severely handicapped students. In a later section of this chapter, more detail is given on the relevant scope and sequence of language development for severely involved students.

Several reports emphasize the generalization of newly acquired language in different environments and with different trainers. Garcia (1974) established conversational speech in severely retarded children through imitation and differential reinforcement across three trainers assigned to three different settings. DeHaven and Garcia (1974) also

Table 6–5. Functional Use of Objects

Behavioral Objective: When presented with target objects, for example, a toothbrush, shoe, comb, or towel, the student will demonstrate the correct use of each object four out of five trials during each session for 3 consecutive days.

Training Procedure:

1. *T* demonstrates by drinking from cup and saying, "Do this." If *S* does not imitate, *T* uses physical prompting. Praise is given for every correct response. *T* varies the use of the objects in as many ways as possible. *T* labels the objects often and uses very simple language while using them. *S* is not required to learn or say these words during this phase.
2. *T* repeats Step 1 for each object.
3. *T* records data on the appropriate sheet.

---

programmed generalized speech usage across several experimenters. Spontaneous question answering by subjects was observed by trainers in this program.

The development of noun production, and at a later point verb production, is a significant aspect of language development in the severely handicapped child. It indicates that the child is now able to self-initiate, that is, spontaneously to request or demand what he or she wants. This may be a verbalization or it may be a demonstration of the eat sign if the child is hungry. In the section below on alternate modes of communication, the production of language is discussed in more detail.

Question-asking skills may be taught once the child begins to produce language regularly. Twardosz and Baer (1973) taught two severely retarded adolescents to ask questions. Token reinforcement was used in conjunction with modeling and fading procedures. Similarly, Swetlik and Brown (1974) trained severely handicapped children to ask "who," "what," and "where" questions. Task analysis sequences were used in presenting the necessary language content. Social reinforcement was given by the teacher for appropriate question-asking behavior.

ALTERNATE MODES OF COMMUNICATION

A potentially fruitful area of research on language programs is the use of gestural or sign language and language boards (Hollis & Carrier, 1975). There have been some studies with severely handicapped children involving sign language (Topper, 1975), communication boards (McDonald & Schultz, 1973), and Bliss symbols (Vanderheiden, Brown, Mackenzie, Reinen, & Schiebel, 1975).

Current nonverbal communications research with primates promises the possibility of new channels of language training for the profoundly handicapped (Fouts, 1973; Gardner & Gardner, 1969; and Premack & Premack, 1972). For example, Premack's work with primates indicated that language can be taught through use of plastic or prosthetic words. To date, a trained primate has learned 130 words, and has progressed through several levels of language sophistication including use of the interrogative, pluralization, simple and compound sentences, if–then statements, class concepts, and the conjunctive *and.* These language parameters have been acquired through operant conditioning techniques.

Manual language may take several forms. A teacher may decide that certain children who are nonverbal might profit from learning simple signs for "eat," "toy," "toilet," and "drink." The use of modified communication boards with a picture exhibited on the board may also be used. As an illustration, consider the possibility of teaching a nonverbal child or a severely physically handicapped student the concept of eat. A picture of several foods could be placed on a piece of 8 X 11 inch cardboard and worn by the child. Table 6–6 outlines instructional sequence for teaching a child how to use a communication board.

Table 6–6. Production of Four Objects on a Communication Board

Pretest Procedures:

Code: 1. Evaluator scores + if student makes correct response.

2. Evaluator scores – if student makes incorrect response.

Criterion: Student demonstrates behavior four out of five trials on 3 successive days.

Phase 1. Functional Use (food, drink, phone, record player)

Objective: S demonstrates appropriate functional use of each object.

Verbal Cue: "Michael, show me what you do with this."

Pretest:

1. Materials: data sheet, table, two chairs, food, drink, phone, record player.
2. *T* places four objects in front of *S* (food, drink, phone, record player with record).
3. *T* gains *S*'s attention by saying, "Look at me," and/or physically guides *S*'s face toward her.
4. *T* points to object and says, "Show me what you do with this."
5. *T* allows *S* 5 seconds to comply.
6. *T* records + if *S* demonstrates behavior.

   T records – if *S* does not demonstrate behavior.
7. A trial terminates when the *S* demonstrates the object's correct function or fails to comply within 5 seconds.
8. *T* continues process for five trials.

Phase 2. Functional Imitation: Communication Board

Objective: S imitates use of board by pointing to picture on board and performing action after trainer.

Verbal Cue: "Michael, do this."

Pretest:

1. Materials: data sheet, two chairs, communication board, food, drink, phone, record player.
2. *T* places board on *S* (food: upper right-hand corner; drink: upper left-hand corner; phone: lower right-hand corner; record player: lower left-hand corner).
3. *T* places communication board on self (pictures of objects in same order).
4. *T* gains *S*'s attention by saying, "Look at me," and guides *S*'s face toward her.

Table 6–6. (Continued)

5. *T* says, "Do this," and hits a corner of the board.
6. *T* allows *S* 5 seconds to comply.
7. *T* records + if *S* demonstrates behavior.
   T records − if *S* does not demonstrate behavior.
8. A trial terminates when *S* demonstrates appropriate imitation or fails to comply within 5 seconds.
9. *T* continues process for five trials.

Phase 3. Comprehension of Communication Board

Objective: *S* identifies picture of object on communication board.

Verbal Cue: "Michael, show me _____ (object name)."

Pretest:

1. Materials: data sheet, communication board, objects: food, drink, phone, record player, two chairs, table.
2. *T* places communication board and objects on table in front of *S*. Communication board is directly in front of *S*.
3. *T* gains *S*'s attention by saying, "Look at me," and guides *S*'s face toward her.
4. *T* points to picture of object on communication board and says, "Michael, show me _____ (object name)."
5. *T* allows *S* 5 seconds to comply.
6. *T* records + for correct response.
   T records − for incorrect response.
7. Trial terminates when *S* identifies the objects or fails to comply within 5 seconds.
8. *T* continues process for five trials.

Phase 4. Production of Communication Board

Objective: *S* indicates need or preference for a given object when placed in an opportunity to initiate response.

Verbal Cue: "Michael, what do you want?" or "Michael, show me what you want."

Pretest:

1. Materials: data sheet, communication board, objects: food, drink, phone, record player, two chairs, table.
2. *T* places communication board on *S*.
3. *T* gains *S*'s attention by saying, "Look at me," and guides *S*'s face toward her.
4. *T* places objects (food, drink, phone, record player) on table in front of *S*.

5. *T* says, "Michael, what do you want?" or "Michael, show me what you want."
6. *T* allows *S* 5 seconds to comply.
7. *T* records + if *S* hits picture on communication board.
   T records − if *S* does not hit picture on communication board or does not make response.
8. Trial terminates when the *S* initiates response or fails to comply within 5 seconds.
9. *T* continues process for five trials.

Decision: Training will begin at the phase of the program on which the student fails to respond 80 to 90 percent of the time (four out of five trials of correct responses on 3 successive days on each phase).

It is relatively simple to construct homemade communication boards. This same training strategy might also be used with severely handicapped blind children by hanging beads around the child's neck; each bead could have a different raised symbol that would stand for different objects. It is better to use this method rather than attempt the more advanced Braille system.

In developing a modified communication board, one should begin with very few objects. They should be objects which the child will likely want to communicate about. The signs for preferred toys and foods would probably be spontaneously produced more readily than objects in which he has little interest. Those readers particularly interested in nonvocal alternatives to speech are referred to an excellent review by Kiernan (1977).

GUIDELINES TO IMPLEMENTING A LANGUAGE DEVELOPMENT PROGRAM

When developing language in individuals with severe behavioral handicaps, it is advantageous to teach from a logical sequence of language skills. This will help determine the appropriate level of skill at which instruction should begin, and will suggest what instructional direction the teacher should take. Although there are few comprehensive programs for children with severe language deficiencies, the language program sequence developed by Bricker and her associates (1976) is an excellent one that is aptly suited to severely and profoundly handicapped students. This section describes the steps involved in implementing this program (Wehman & Garrett, in press).

Program Implementation

RATIONALE FOR SELECTION OF A LANGUAGE PROGRAM.   Many experimental studies describe language research with severely handicapped persons (e.g., Snyder, Lovitt, & Smith, 1975), and many programs are commercially available (Kent, 1973). Unfortunately, few easy to understand programs which could be implemented with relatively little difficulty were found.

The program developed by Bricker, Ruder, and Vincent[1] (1976), however, was selected for review because it features several critical characteristics. First, it is written in language that teachers can understand and grasp with a minimum of difficulty. Second, its developmental sequence and logic are attractive in that they allow teachers to go to the lowest possible level of language intervention, attending, all the way through considerably more advanced stages of language. Third, provisions built into the program ensure transfer of training; this is a critical component because transfer cannot be assumed to be spontaneous in severely handicapped students (Wehman, Abramson, & Norman, 1977). Finally, this language sequence has been

[1]A somewhat revised edition of this program can be obtained from Dr. Diane Bricker at the Center on Human Development, University of Oregon, Eugene, Oregon.

empirically verified by earlier research (Bricker, Dennison, Watson, & Vincent, 1973).

INITIAL ASSESSMENT.   Students can be assessed in the following way: For each student, the language therapist gathers baseline data for several days across phases of the language program thought to be relevant for that student. For example, some children may not be capable of even the simplest prerequisite—paying attention for 1 or 2 seconds —and therefore no further baseline data would be gathered. On the other hand, many students will demonstrate limited proficiency on one or more of the beginning phases in the program. Because of this inconsistency it may be best to assess several phases of the program before pinpointing the appropriate entry level skill.

REVIEW OF ASSESSMENT DATA.   The initial assessment stage usually takes several weeks to complete. A standard criterion that can be established for proficiency in a given phase is 80 percent of the trials for three consecutive days. At the end of the assessment period, each child will be placed in the phase of the language program to where he or she can no longer meet criterion. Many of the students in the target group may require prerequisite instruction in attending and motor imitation.

DATA COLLECTION PROCEDURES.   Data should be collected each day. During baseline assessment and instructional sessions, a probe method of data collection can be used during each session. For example, instruction will take place for a designated length of time. At the end of that time, the language therapist might say "Data time," and each teacher would present the student(s) with whom he or she was working five trials for criterion performance. If the student responds correctly, only social reinforcement such as "good" would be given and (a+) would be recorded on the data sheet. No response or inappropriate responses would earn an (a–). This daily assessment would be recorded on graphs for each child. Criterion would be four of five correct responses, or 80 percent, for three consecutive days.

INSTRUCTIONAL PROCEDURES.   The basic instructional model consists of instructions, modeling, prompting and fading, and reinforcement. For each trial the teacher will give the appropriate cue for the child to perform. If the child responds correctly, reinforcement should be given immediately. Positive reinforcement should always include praise and affection, and edible reinforcers such as Fruit Loops or Pepsi-Cola may be used frequently. If the student does not respond correctly or fails to respond, the response may be modeled. A correct response should then be followed by reinforcement. If the child still does not respond appropriately, the teacher can try physical priming of the target behavior.

An important part of this training sequence, particularly in the initial stages of instruction, is to identify correct approximations of the desired response. These approximations can then be reinforced in an effort to shape the correct behavior.

Table 6–7 lists the prerequisite skills and first 16 phases in the Bricker (1976) language sequence. The instructional cue which the teacher gives to start the training sequence is also listed. These phases are specified because they are the most characteristic of language content for severely and profoundly handicapped students.

One session per day can be conducted for each child, with different time periods blocked out for each class. The language therapist should coordinate all language activities through the teachers, be directly involved in instruction each day, and also coordinate data collection. Language sessions are usually possible with a teacher-to-student ratio of one-to-two or one-to-three, but in some cases one-to-one instruction is required. An effort should be made to

**Table 6–7. Summary of the Bricker Language Program:
Prerequisite Skills and First Phases**

Phase	*Cue*
Prerequisite 1. Sitting in a chair	"S, sit in the chair."
Prerequisite 2. Attending	"S, look at me."
Prerequisite 3. Motor imitation	"S, do this."
Phase 1. Functional use of objects	"S, show me what you do with this."
Phase 2. Verbal imitation of sounds	"S, say _____."
Phase 3. Comprehension of nouns	"Give me (show me, touch, etc.) the _____."
Phase 4. Verbal imitation of nouns	"S, say _____."
Phase 5. Production of nouns	"What's this?"
Phase 6. Verbal imitation of verbs	"S, say _____."
Phase 7. Comprehension of verbs	"Make it _____," or "Make her _____."
Phase 8. Production of verbs	"What's it doing?" or "What's going on?"
Phase 9. Imitation of two-word phrases	"S, say _____ _____."
Phase 10. Comprehension of two-word phrases	"Fill truck," or "Push car."
Phase 11. Production of two-word phrases	"What am I doing?" or "What's happening?"
Phase 12. Imitation of three-word phrases	"S, say _____ _____ _____ (agent) (verb) (object)"
Phase 13. Production of three-word phrases	"What's going on?" or "What am I doing"
Phase 14. Comprehension of modified nouns	"Give me (show me, touch, etc.) the _____ _____." (red) (car)

use different materials and trainers during the language session to prepare for transfer of training.

The total school staff should be included in a language program, and, in fact, may be required to attend in-service training by the language therapist.

MONITORING DATA AND EVALUATION. Data must be plotted on graphs daily for each child. This allows immediate feedback on the progress which each child is making. By periodically evaluating the children in each class, the reinforcers being given can be modified, and the types of tasks being used to teach the target language skill can be altered. This type of direct evaluation provides the teacher with an objective measure of what gains the students are making.

IN-SERVICE TRAINING. Periodic in-service training sessions for the staff can include the following measures:

1. Passing out copies of the program and describing it in detail so that all involved know the logic and rationale behind it.
2. Giving demonstrations for how to shape low-level language skills.
3. Having staff role-play and rehearse the appropriate behaviors.
4. Passing out information describing how to record data and then making sure that all staff has practice in data collection.

In addition, a general rule can be made that only those who receive in-service training may be involved in language training sessions. This minimizes difficulties caused by a nonuniform approach to the program.

Sequence, structure, and objective evaluation measures in language instruction will ensure that most severely handicapped children will begin to acquire functional language skills. A comprehensive program guarantees uniformity from classroom to classroom, and thereby facilitates communication and discussion among teachers, parents, and administrators. Furthermore, when the language therapist is given greater responsibility in the language program, rather than serving only as a consultant to teachers or taking a handful of students off to the "language room," the children will benefit more.

EVALUATION OF LANGUAGE RESEARCH

Modeling, prompting and fading, and positive reinforcement are the principal components of language development with the severely and profoundly handicapped. Snyder et al. (1975) reviewed 23 language studies, and each utilized some form of imitation as a means of establishing communication.

Most of the language studies reviewed were experimentally valid, reliable, and rigorously evaluated in reversal or multiple baseline designs. Unfortunately, a major limitation is the small number of subjects involved in most of these studies; for example, only 64 subjects participated in the 23 studies reviewed by Snyder.

In their review of language research, Garcia and DeHaven (1974) conclude that an operant technology clearly exists for the establishment and maintenance of expressive speech. Their analysis of the research suggested six excellent target areas for future investigation (p. 177):

1. The relationship of motor imitation to vocal imitation for training.
2. The function of each component used during vocal imitative development and later speech acquisition (shaping, fading, chaining).
3. Exact specification of training techniques (e.g., shaping) in some standard manner.
4. Analysis of the development, limits, and maintenance of appropriate speech generalization (defined procedurally or functionally), and the

generative response class properties with respect to speech development.

5. Analysis of both the subjects that succeeded and those that failed in language research.

6. Practical issues concerning the necessity of a one-to-one relationship and the use of highly trained receptive speech to those individuals with severe verbal deficiencies who would otherwise require a long history of training in productive speech.

SUMMARY

There is little doubt that if severely and profoundly handicapped persons are unable to communicate their needs, the success of current movements toward deinstitutionalization and community integration will be diminished. From this brief review of research, it is evident that an instructional technology is available for the development of expressive and receptive language skills in individuals with severe communication deficits. Future work must be directed at disseminating this information to trained professionals and parents.

REFERENCES

Baer, D., & Guess, D. Receptive training of adjectival inflections in mental retardates. *Journal of Applied Behavior Analysis,* 1971, *4,* 129–139.

Barton, E. S. Inappropriate speech in a severely retarded child: A case study in language conditioning and generalization. *Journal of Applied Behavior Analysis,* 1970, *3,* 299–307.

Barton, E. S. Operant conditioning of social speech in the severely subnormal and the use of different reinforcers. *British Journal of Social and Clinical Psychology,* 1972, *11,* 387–391.

Bricker, D., Ruder, K., & Vincent, B. An intervention strategy for language deficient children. Chapter 9 in N. Haring & R. Schiefebusch (Eds.), *Teaching special children*. New York: McGraw-Hill, 1976, 300–341.

Brown, L., Bellamy, G. T., Tang, P. & Klemme, H. A procedure for teaching trainable students to follow verbal directions. Unpublished manuscript, Department of Studies in Behavioral Disabilities, University of Wisconsin, 1971.

Bry, P., & Nawas, M. Is reinforcement necessary for the development of a generalization imitation operant in severely and profoundly retarded children? *American Journal of Mental Deficiency*, 1972, *76(6)*, 658–667.

Craighead, W. C., O'Leary, K., & Allen, J. Teaching and generalization of instruction-following in an "autistic" child. *Journal of Behavior Therapy and Experimental Psychiatry*, 1973, *4(2)*, 171–176.

DeHaven, E., & Garcia, E. Continuation of training as a variable influencing the generalization of speech in a nonverbal retardate. Paper presented at the meeting of the Rocky Mountain Psychological Association, Denver, May 1974.

Fouts, R. S. Acquisition and testing of gestural signs in four young chimpanzees. *Science*, 1973, *180*, 978–980.

Garcia, E. The training and generalization of a conversational speech form in nonverbal retardates. *Journal of Applied Behavior Analysis*, 1974, *7*, 137–151.

Garcia, E., & DeHaven, E. Use of operant techniques in the establishment and generalization of language: A review and analysis. *American Journal of Mental Deficiency*, 1974, *79*, 169–178.

Garcia, E., Baer, D. M., & Firestone, I. The development of generalized imitation within topographically determined boundaries. *Journal of Applied Behavior Analysis*, 1971, *4*, 101–113.

Garcia, E., Guess, D., & Byrnes, J. Development of syntax in a retarded girl using procedures of imitation, reinforcement, and modeling. *Journal of Applied Behavior Analysis*, 1973, *6*, 299–311.

Gardner, R., & Gardner, B. Teaching sign language to a chimpanzee. *Science*, 1969, *165*, 664–672.

Griffiths, H., & Craighead, W. Generalization in operant speech therapy for misarticulation. *Journal of Speech and Hearing Disorders*, 1972, *37(1)*, 485–493.

Guess, D. A functional analysis of receptive language and productive speech: Acquisition of the plural morpheme. *Journal of Applied Behavior Analysis*, 1969, *2*, 55–64.

Guess, D., & Baer, D. An analysis of individual differences in generalization between receptive and productive language in retarded children. *Journal of Applied Behavior Analysis,* 1973, *6,* 311–329.

Guess, D., Sailor, W., Rutherford, G., & Baer, D. M. An experimental analysis of linguistic development: The productive use of the plural morpheme. *Journal of Applied Behavior Analysis,* 1968, *1,* 297–306.

Hollis, J., & Carrier, J. Research implications for communication deficiencies. *Exceptional Children,* 1975, *41,* 405–412.

Jeffrey, D. B. Increase and maintenance of verbal behavior of a mentally retarded child. *Mental Retardation,* 1972, *10(2),* 35–39.

Kiernan, C. Alternatives to speech: A review of research on manual and other forms of communication with the mentally handicapped and other non-communicating populations. *British Journal of Mental Subnormality,* June, 1977, 6–28.

Kircher, A., Pear, J., & Martin, G. L. Shock as punishment in a picture-naming task with retarded children. *Journal of Applied Behavior Analysis,* 1971, *4,* 227–233.

Lawrence, J. A. A comparison of operant methodologies relative to language development in the institutionalized mentally retarded. Boston University School of Education, 1971. *Dissertation Abstracts International,* 1971, *32A,* 1943–1944.

Lloyd, L. (Ed.). *Communication assessment and intervention strategies.* Baltimore, Maryland: University Park Press, 1976.

MacAulay, B. A program for teaching speech and beginning reading to nonverbal retardates. In H. N. Sloane, Jr., & B. MacAulay (Eds.), *Operant procedures in remedial speech and language training.* Boston: Houghton-Mifflin, 1968.

McDonald, E., & Schultz, A. Communication boards for cerebral palsied children. *General Speech and Hearing Disorders,* 1973, *38,* 73–88.

Peine, H., Gregersen, G., & Sloane, H. A program to increase vocabulary and spontaneous verbal behavior. *Mental Retardation,* 1970, *8(2),* 38–44.

Premack, A. J., & Premack, D. Teaching language to an ape. *Scientific American,* 1972, *277,* 92–99.

Sailor, W. Reinforcement and generalization of productive plural allomorphs in two retarded children. *Journal of Applied Behavior Analysis,* 1971, *4,* 305–310.

Schroeder, G., & Baer, D. M. Effects of concurrent and serial training on generalized vocal imitation in retarded children. *Developmental Psychology,* 1972, *6,* 293–301.

Schumaker, J., & Sherman, J. Training generative verb usage by imitation and reinforcement procedures. *Journal of Applied Behavior Analysis,* 1970, *3,* 273–287.

Sloane, H., Johnston, M., & Harris, F. Remedial procedures for teaching verbal behavior to speech deficient and defective young children. In

H. N. Sloane & B. MacAulay (Eds.), *Operant procedures in remedial speech and language training.* Boston: Houghton-Mifflin, 1968.

Snyder, L., Lovitt, T., & Smith, J. Language training with the severely retarded: Five years of applied behavior analysis research. *Exceptional Children,* 1975, *42,* 8–15.

Stewart, F. A vocal-motor program for teaching nonverbal children. *Education and Training of the Mentally Retarded,* 1972, *7,* 176–182.

Streifel, S. *Teaching a child to imitate.* Lawrence, Kansas: H and H Enterprises, Inc., 1974.

Streifel, S., & Weatherby, B. Instruction-following behavior of a retarded child and its controlling stimuli. *Journal of Applied Behavior Analysis,* 1976, *6(4),* 663–670.

Swetlik, B., & Brown, L. Teaching severely handicapped students to express selected first, second, and third person singular pronoun responses in answer to "who-doing" questions. In L. Brown, W. Williams, & T. Crowner (Eds.), *A collection of papers and programs related to public school services for severely handicapped students.* Madison, Wisconsin: Madison Public School System, 1974.

Topper, S. Gesture language for a nonverbal severely retarded male. *Mental Retardation,* 1975, *13,* 30–31.

Twardosz, S., & Baer, D. M. Training two severely retarded adolescents to ask questions. *Journal of Applied Behavior Analysis,* 1973, *6,* 655–661.

Vanderheiden, D., Brown, W., Mackenzie, P., Reinen, S., & Schiebel, F. Symbol communication for the mentally handicapped. *Mental Retardation,* 1975, *13,* 34–37.

Waldron, F. Developing techniques to facilitate instruction following behaviors in a classroom for mentally retarded students. *Education and Training of the Mentally Retarded,* 1975, *10(4),* 262–267.

Wehman, P., Schutz, R., Renzaglia, A., & Karan, O. Use of positive practice to facilitate increased work productivity and instruction following behavior in profoundly retarded adolescents. In O. C. Karan, P. Wehman, A. Renzaglia, & R. Schutz (Eds.), *Habilitation practices with the severely developmentally disabled.* Madison, Wisconsin: University of Wisconsin Rehabilitation Research and Training Center, 1977.

Wehman, P., & Garrett, S. Language instruction with the severely, profoundly and multi-handicapped: two years of data. *Mental Retardation,* in press.

Whitman, T. L., Zakaras, M., & Chardos, S. Effects of reinforcement and guidance procedures on instruction following behavior in retarded children. *Journal of Applied Behavior Analysis,* 1971, *4,* 283–291.

Chapter 7

FUNCTIONAL ACADEMICS

This chapter evaluates the literature on functional academics with severely handicapped students. At one point it was thought that the severely handicapped were not capable of learning academic skills, and that self-care and simple language were the only skills they could be expected to develop (Sloan & Birch, 1955). Fortunately, work by Brown and his associates (e.g., Brown, Williams & Crowner, 1974) has begun to dispell this notion.

Brown and York (1974) noted that, with the national impetus toward education for all handicapped children, special educators must deliver quality education. They believe that special education has a responsibility to train functional academics to the severely handicapped, and that if public schools act only baby sitters, the potential for backlash from taxpayers will be great:

> If it can be demonstrated that a child who was once tied to a bed in an institution because he or she was self-mutilating

can now read, write, compute, socialize, and in other ways
behave adaptively, few people will complain about giving up
a new chemistry lab, new football uniforms, or small portions of their salary increases. If, on the other hand, a child
who was once tied to a bed in an institution is now tied to
a bed in a public school classroom, it is doubtful that many
persons will graciously accept the aforementioned economic
adjustments. Obviously, the example of the child tied to a
bed was used to dramatize a point. However, children sitting
in classrooms fingerpainting for ten months is less dramatic
but will probably make the same point to the economically
strapped taxpayer. (Brown & York, 1974, p. 3)

Given the present state of fiscal affairs in many state
and local education agencies, the practical utility of Brown
and York's philosophy should be evident. Although some
severely and profoundly handicapped students have more
pressing needs, such as toilet training or even swallowing,
there are many who may be able to develop a certain level
of proficiency in basic preacademic and academic skills.
This review primarily concerns literature and programs in
basic arithmetic and reading.

Basic Arithmetic Skills

To function with any independence on jobs or in community facilities, one must have some competence in arithmetic. If the severely handicapped are to function effectively
in a community, they must be able to use basic math concepts and operations. For example, the student must be
able to use money, tell time, understand a time schedule,
and read recipes for measurement.

Brown (1973) observed that if severely handicapped
students are to acquire basic math skills, a tenable sequence
of skills must first be generated. Secondly, an effective technology for teaching the components of math skills sequences must be developed. However, he states that

"there is meager information to which a teacher of trainable
level retarded students can turn for help on how to teach
basic mathematical skills. The available information is in-
complete, unsystematic, cross-sectional, and for the most
part lacking in empirical verification." (p. 8)

A review of the literature on the development of basic
arithmetic skills in severely handicapped students essentially supports this position. A computer search performed
through the ERIC system retrieved a large number of arithmetic training programs completed with lower-functioning
retarded students. Most of the programs did not specify
replicable teaching procedures or did not specifically manipulate learning variables that might influence the instructional situation.

What was discovered was the effectiveness of task analysis and the structured reinforcement procedures that
Brown and his colleagues have used in recent years to teach
arithmetic. For example, Bellamy and Brown (1972) reported instructional procedures that gave a group of trainable level retarded students the skills necessary to add any
two numbers that totaled 10 or less. Components of this
program, which were taught individually, and then chained
together into a sequence, included (1) labeling printed
numbers from 1 to 10, (2) writing numerals from a verbal
cue, (3) counting and drawing quantities of lines corresponding to printed numberals, (4) counting quantities of
lines and writing the total, and (5) completing preaddition
exercises.

Similar task analysis sequences have been developed
for addition and subtraction (Bellamy, Greiner, & Buttars,
1974), counting objects (Brown, Bellamy, & Gadberry,
1971; Coleman, 1970), and counting money (Bellamy &
Laffin, 1974). Table 7–1 lists the specific steps and teaching
procedures reported by Bellamy and Laffin (1974) in teaching severely handicapped students to count money.

Table 7–1. Instructional Program for Counting Money

Task 1: Rote Counting to 100

A. Instructional cue: *T*'s verbal instruction, "Count to 100," is presented without teaching materials.

B. Task requirement and measurement: *S* must voice all numerals 1 through 100 in sequence. Numerals voiced in sequence before the first error are considered correct.

C. Teaching consequence: If *S* counts correctly, *T* and other *Ss* compliment him and he earns 2 points on his point card. If *S* does not reach 100, but his last correct response is better (i.e., *S* counts further) than on the previous trial, he receives 1 point. If *S* miscounts, *T* stops him as soon as the error occurs and models the correct response (e.g., "After 36 comes 37"). Then *T* says, "What comes after 36?" One or two repetitions of this procedure are consistently sufficient to produce the desired response. Then *T* says, "Begin at _____ (e.g., 30, or the previous even 10) and count on."

Task 2: Counting by 5s to 100

A. Instructional cue: *T*'s verbal instruction, "Count by 5s to 100," is presented without teaching materials.

B. Task requirement and measurement: *S* must count by 5s to 100. Numerals voiced in sequence before the first error are considered correct.

C. Teaching consequence: If *S* counts correctly, *T* and other *Ss* compliment him and he receives points for correct responding or improvement, as in Task 1. If *S* miscounts, *T* stops him as soon as the error occurs and models the correct response (e.g., "After 30 comes 35"). *T* then asks, "What comes after _____" (*S*'s last correct response), and repeats the model when necessary until *S* responds correctly.

Task 3: Counting by 10s to 100

A. Instructional cue: *T*'s verbal instruction, "Count by 10s to 100," is presented without teaching materials.

B. Task requirement and measurement: *S* must count by 10s to 100. Numerals voiced in sequence before the first error are considered correct.

C. Teaching consequence: If *S* counts correctly, *T* and other *Ss* compliment him and he receives points for correct responding or improvement, as in previous tasks. If *S* miscounts, *T* uses modeling, as in previous tasks, until *S* gives a correct or improved response.

223

Table 7–1. (Continued)

Task 4: Counting by 25s to 100

A. Instructional cue: *T*'s verbal instruction, "Count by 25s to 100," is presented without teaching materials.

B. Task requirement and measurement: *S* must count by 25s to 100. Numerals voiced in sequence before the first error are considered correct.

C. Teaching consequence: If *S* miscounts, *T* uses modeling as in previous tasks, until *S* gives a correct or improved response.

Task 5: Labeling Price Cards

A. Instructional cue: *T*'s verbal instruction, "What does this card say?" is presented with each of the 100 price cards.

B. Task requirement and measurement: *S* must voice the numeral and label the cents sign that appears on each price card (e.g., "twenty-four cents"). All price cards labeled correctly by *Ss* are recorded as correct. During baseline, but not during teaching trials, a price card is counted as correct if *S*'s only error is failure to label the cents sign.

C. Teaching consequence: If *S* correctly reads all the cards missed previously, *T* and other *Ss* compliment him and he receives 2 points on his point card. One point is assigned for improving previous performance. If *S* misreads a card, *T* models the correct response (e.g., "The card says 36 cents. What does it say?") until *S* responds appropriately. Cards labeled correctly by all *Ss* on two consecutive trials are no longer taught.

Task 6: Identifying Coins

A. Instructional cue: *T*'s verbal instruction, "Touch the (penny, nickel, dime, quarter)," is presented with one of each of the coins.

B. Task requirement and measurement: *S* must touch the coin indicated by *T*. All coins correctly touched by *Ss* are recorded as correct.

C. Teaching consequence: If *S* responds correctly, *T* and other *Ss* compliment him and he receives 1 point. If *S* is incorrect, *T* models the correct response (i.e., points to the requested coin), and then repeats the initial instruction. (All *Ss* have responded correctly after *T*'s model.)

Task 7: Counting Amounts of Money on Price Cards (Sets a–j)

A. Instructional cue: *T*'s verbal instruction, "Read the card and count out that much money," is presented with each price card in a set. The set of coins containing four of each coin is on the table in front of *S*.

Table 7–1. (Continued)

B. Task requirement and measurement: S must read the price card and count out the amount of change indicated. A response is recorded as correct when both the reading and counting responses are correct.

C. Teaching consequences: If S counts correctly, he is complimented by T and other Ss and earns 1 point on his point card. Points are also assigned at the end of each trial for increases above previous trials. A variety of errors are possible on this task; the type of error committed determines the specific teaching procedures employed. If S misreads a price card, the modeling procedures described in Task 5 are used until the card is correctly labeled. T then repeats the instruction, "Count out that much money." If S does not count correctly, T first instructs him to "Count by ____" (1s, 5s, 10s, 25s), and then repeats the initial instruction. If S still miscounts, T models the desired verbal response (e.g., for 68 cents, "25–50–60–65–66–67–68") but does not touch the coins. The initial instruction is repeated. If S fails to respond correctly after this procedure, or if S counts correctly but fails to move appropriate coins, T asks S to count as T moves coins in the proper sequence for the particular price card. If S fails to respond correctly after the above procedures, T models the entire response, then repeats the initial instruction. (One or two repetitions of this model consistently produce the correct response.)

Adapted by permission of Bellamy and Buttars (1974) and *Education and Training of the Mentally Retarded.*

Each of these programs employed a basic instructional model. The instructions were given, then followed by a verbal model or physical assistance if an incorrect response was made. Correct responses were followed immediately with either edible reinforcement or social reinforcement from the teacher. Although this approach has been effective in training basic arithmetic skills, several limitations are evident: (1) Small samples of students participated in the programs. (2) Not all the students achieved the terminal objective, although most made some progress. (3) The time involved was sometimes quite long. (4) Many of the programs were not evaluated in rigorous experimental designs.

Task analysis and reinforcement might be further enhanced by manipulation of general learning variables that influence all types of learning and not only operant conditioning. One example of this was demonstrated by Lovitt and Curtiss (1969) with an emotionally disturbed boy who made many errors in arithmetic problems. By instructing the child to recite aloud as he completed the problems, they increased both accuracy and performance rate.

Another general learning variable that has been manipulated is knowledge of results. Through a fixed ratio of praise and immediate feedback of correct answers, a nonretarded junior high school student was trained to increase the number of arithmetic problems he completed (Kirby & Shields, 1972). Token reinforcement (Ferritor, Buckholdt, Hamblin, & Smith, 1972) and self-reinforcement (Lovitt & Curtiss, 1968) have been also used to increase arithmetic performance rates.

A math skills curriculum directed toward severely handicapped students has been developed by Williams, Coyne, Johnson, Scheuerman, Stepner, & Swetlik (1974). This curriculum serves as a guideline for selecting the appropriate entry level skills for students. Table 7–2 details the scope and sequence of objectives on the curriculum.

Resnick, Wang, and Kaplan (1973) developed a similar curricular based on work with nonretarded preschoolers. This curriculum also involved a task analytic approach to math skill development.

These curriculum efforts provide excellent models for *what* to teach, and in *what sequence* to teach. However, they do not provide explicit instruction about *how* to teach or how to present a given skill to encourage the best response from students. No curriculum can do this; only effective teaching technology can meet this need.

This brief review of the literature on basic arithmetic skills indicates little controlled research had been devoted to evaluating the effectiveness of different instructional

Table 7–2. Scope and Sequence Chart for Math Curriculum

	Objectives															
A. Prerequisites																
1. Motor imitation	1															
2. Verbal imitation		1	2													
B. Sets		1	2	3	4	5	6	7	8	9						
C. One-to-one correspondence				1	2	3										
D. Equality					1	2	3	4								
E. One–many				1	2	3										
F. More and less																
1. More						1										
2. Less							1	2								
3. More/less									1	2						
G. Counting																
1. Rational				1	2	3	4									
2. Rote							1	2	3							
3. Numeral recognition							1									
4. Matching numerals to quantities							1									
5. Matching quantities to numerals							1									
6. Ordering quantities								1								
7. Ordering numerals									1	2						
H. Addition																
1. Objects							1	2	3							
2. Numerals and objects									1							
3. Numerals and lines										1						
4. Numerals											1					
5. Fingers												1	2	3	4	
6. Facts											1	2	3	4	5	6

Reprinted with the kind permission of Williams et al. (1974).

variables. Most of the studies reported included a sample too small to support generalizations. Most programs focused on demonstrating the efficacy of task analysis and manipulation of consequence conditions. Too few studies examined the effects of manipulating different antecedent events in an arithmetic training situation.

Although a good start has been made, instructional guidelines for teaching basic math skills need greater development and verification. A substantial challenge to educators is finding tasks, games, and activities that can be used to math skills to lower functioning handicapped students. The curriculum work of Williams and his coworkers needs to be validated to verify that the instructional sequence is appropriate. Math skill training must move out of the classroom and into functional community settings such as stores, vocational centers, and restaurants.

BASIC READING SKILLS

Although the utility of teaching reading to trainable retarded and severely handicapped students has been a controversial issue (Apfel, 1975; Brown, 1973; Burton, 1974; Goldberg & Rooke, 1967), I believe reading can be successfully taught to the severely handicapped. Recent pioneering work by Brown and associates (1974, 1975) supports the reading potential of severely handicapped students:

> If it is a tenable assumption that basic reading skills are crucial to survival in a community setting, then there are at least three instructional issues that must be confronted. First, are trainable level retarded students intellectually capable of learning to read to such an extent that they can function in a community setting? Second, what specific reading content should be taught? Third, *how* should reading be taught? . . . The problem, however, is that the professional

community has not yet delineated and empirically verified
the instructional procedures to teach the necessary skills.
(Brown, 1973, p. 8)

A whole word approach seems to be the most effective
and economical way to teach reading to the severely handicapped. Although the phonetic approach has been tried
with trainable retarded students (MacAulay, 1968), it is
clear that the more successful programs have involved
whole word training. Therefore, a brief review of these
efforts is described below.

Brown and his colleagues (1973) developed an initial
sight work reading and alphabet skill program by presenting material in a task analysis format. Modeling and priming were used, with praise given for correct responses. This
instructional model has been employed to develop functional reading skills (Brown & Perlmutter, 1971), reading
comprehension (Domnie & Brown, 1974), chart story reading (Johnson & Brown, 1974), and unconjugated action
verbs (Brown, Huppler, Pierce, York, & Sontag, 1974).
Functional reading was operationally defined as a two-step
sequence in which a student (1) verbally labeled a printed
stimulus, and (2) responded differentially to the printed
stimulus, i.e., by pairing a picture with the appropriate
word.

Stimulus fading is a variable that has received some
attention in the development of reading skills in retarded
students. Dorry and Zeaman (1973) give one application of
fading to word attack skills:

A picture and corresponding printed word are presented
stimultaneously, with the result that the responses to the
printed word are learned with repeated pairings. When a
fading procedure is applied to the simultaneous pairing of
picture and word, the picture is gradually faded out with
each repeated pairing while the word remains fully visible.
(p. 3)

Using this method, Dorry and Zeaman (1973) developed word acquisition skills in trainable retarded children. More words were learned with the fading method than with a nonfading method, and the fading method also resulted in greater transfer of training to a second list. Similar results have been obtained in laboratory settings (Sidman & Stoddard, 1967; Sidman & Cresson, 1973).

Token and edible reinforcement have also been used to teach sight words and to increase attending to reading tasks by Staats and his colleagues (Staats & Butterfield, 1965; Staats, Minke, Goodwin, & Landeen, 1967). Similarly, penny reinforcement has been used to increase comprehension in mildly retarded children (Lahey, NcNees, & Brown, 1976). For a more definitive review of reading research with handicapped children, the reader is referred to Wehman (1977).

It should be evident from this review that discrimination learning and reinforcement theory have been basic to most of the successful efforts at teaching reading to lower functioning handicapped students. Yet if it can be demonstrated that the verbal and conceptual learning variable manipulations (Blake, 1973; 1975; 1976) used with EMR students are valid with severely handicapped students, then a more powerful instructional technology might be established. This could be done by collating the research literature on operant conditioning, verbal learning, and concept learning.

PREWRITING SKILLS

Writing is a developmental process that can be facilitated by training students in fine motor skills. The student must have gross and fine manual and arm control, and must be able to focus on the drawing material.

Writing is important for the severely handicapped because (1) it is essential in filling out medical and job applications forms, and in communicating with friends; (2) it improves recognition of words and numbers; and (3) it improves overall eye-hand coordination.

Although there is too little teaching of prewriting skills to trainable retarded and severely handicapped students, Brown, Scheuerman, Cartwright, and York (1973) determined several behavioral objectives in this area:

1. *Ss* were to produce specified stroke elements when presented with a printed model of the desired stroke.
2. *Ss* were to combine the appropriate strokes elements to form the letters in their first names when presented with a printed model of the specific letters.
3. *Ss* were to combine the appropriate letters in the correct sequence to print their first names when presented with a printed model of their name. (p. 200)

The end goal of prewriting is that the child use visual-motor control to produce configurations with definite meaning or purpose. This means that the student transcends scribbling and progresses to the production of geometric figures. The drawing of lines, circles, triangles, crosses, and squares is practical because they make up the basic forms of the English alphabet. Table 7–3 outlines a prewriting instructional sequence program.

Summary

This discussion of functional academics has been necessarily brief. There are only a few instructional programs in this curriculum area for lower functioning handicapped students. Furthermore, severely handicapped students typically have more pressing needs in self-help, social, lan-

Table 7–3. Prewriting Instructional Sequence

Large Muscle Activity

A. *Free scribbling*

Objective: When given a piece of chalk and while standing in front of the chalkboard, the student will make some mark on the board at least 2 inches in length or diameter.

Materials: Oversized chalk, chalkboard.

Child's desired action	Teacher's action
1. Grasps piece of chalk.	1. Hands chalk to S saying, "Hold the chalk."
2. Faces the chalkboard.	2. Says, "Look at the board."
3. Brings hand with chalk to the board.	3. Says, "Marie, draw on the board."
4. Moves arm in any direction any number of times, having the chalk make contact with the board.	4. Says, "Good drawing," with a touch on the shoulder, a pat on the back, or a smile.

For each step, if the child doesn't attend to the verbal cue, the teacher repeats it. Then, if necessary, a model performs the correct action. If that doesn't work, physical assistance is given along with instruction. As each step is attained, the child is verbally reinforced, but if he or she is slow or on lower functioning level, food may be used for reinforcement after each step is attained (continuous reinforcement). Once the steps are being learned, intermittent reinforcement can be used so that the child must perform more than one step to receive reinforcement. These procedures are also used with making the push-pull stroke described below.

The type of data recording used here and for the remaining task analyses is a frequency count. For each trial a plus (if the task is done independently) or a minus (if the student needs some assistance) is marked by each step in the task analysis.

B. *Making a push-pull stroke*

Objective: The student will draw a line with a crayon on newsprint from a starting point to a brightly colored block all in one motion at least 5 times.

Materials: A large, brightly colored crayon, newsprint, and a brightly colored block or some other attractable object.

Prerequisites: The newsprint is taped to the desk or table so that it won't move around. The child is seated in front of the paper.

232

Child's desired action	Teacher's action
1. Picks up the crayon.	1. Says, "Pick up crayon."
2. Brings the crayon point onto the paper	2. Says, "Touch the paper."
3. Either pushes or pulls hand across the paper, making a line to where the block is.	3. Says, "Catch me," or "Catch this."
4. Repeats step 3 four more times.	4. Once S connects the line from the last point to the block, T says, "Oops, I got away. Catch me."

A nice variation of block or object following is using a moving light beam from a penlight. The light is tapped to get the attention of the child and is then moved across a dark paper which the child follows with a light crayon or marker. This exercise can also be varied by using such surface materials as rolled out clay and a stylus, a sand tray, or finger paints. These textured surfaces add an extra sensory dimension for those who have trouble moving their hand to a goal. They can see and feel the desired direction with these special materials.

More Controlled Direction

A. *Drawing a circle*

Objective: Without a stencil, the student will draw 10 circles (a curved line with connected ends) within the confines of the stimulus area on the paper.

Materials: Large crayon or marker, five pieces of white square paper —8, 5, 3, 1, and 1/4 inch wide—pasted onto a larger piece of 12-inch square colored paper, and five stencils of heavy, clear 12-inch plastic with the outer line of circles whose diameters are 8, 5, 3, 1, and 1/4 inches wide cut out and centered in the squares of plastic.

Prerequisites: The plastic stencils are paperclipped over the corresponding width of white paper. The teacher has the stencil in position over the appropriate stimulus paper. The child is sitting with the paper and stencil directly before her or him and a large, soft pencil or colored thin marker to her or his dominant side of the paper.

Child's desired action	Teacher's action
1. Picks up the pencil.	1. Says, "Pick up the pencil."
2. Moves the pencil point into the top right of the circle form.	2. Says, "Put the pencil on circle."

233

Table 7–3. (Continued)

Child's desired behavior	Teacher's action
3. Moving in counterclockwise motion, draws a circle.	3. Says, "Draw a circle."

At first, physical assistance is given with each step. It is later faded when the child draws her or his own circle in the stencil. After 10 circles have been drawn with the stencil, the stencil is taken away and the child is asked to draw a circle on the white paper. When each circle is correctly drawn without a stencil 10 times, the child may progress to the next smaller stencil. The target behavior is to draw a 1/4-inch circle independently. Continuous social or paired social and edible reinforcement are given at first after each correct step. Reinforcement is faded and ultimately given only after 10 circles are independently drawn. All of the above procedures are followed for the remainder of the tasks: simple cross, X, square, V, and triangle.

B. *Drawing a simple cross* (+)

Objective: Without a stencil, the student will draw 10 simple crosses within the confines of the stimulus area on the paper.

Materials: Exactly the same as the above circle materials, except that lines are cut out to form simple crosses whose lines are 8, 5, 3, 1, and 1/4 inch long (one cross per stencil).

Prerequisites: Same as for circle.

Child's desired behavior	*Teacher's action*
1. Picks up the pencil.	1. Says, "Pick up the pencil."
2. Positions the pencil point into the top of the vertical line.	2. Says, "Put the pencil on the cross."
3. Moves hand downward to the end of line, making the vertical line.	3. Says, "Draw a cross."
4. Picks up hand and moves it to the far left of the horizontal line.	
5. Moves hand toward right, drawing the horizontal line.	

C. *Drawing an X*

Objective: Without a stencil, the student will draw 10 Xs within the confines of the stimulus area on the paper.

Materials: Same as circle, but with Xs of 8, 5, 3, 1, and 1/4 inch lines.

Prerequisites: Same as for circle.

The steps are basically the same as above. The figure is made by always moving left to right. Begin with the diagonal line that starts at the upper left and moves to the lower right, then go to the diagonal line that starts at the lower left and moves to the upper right.

D. *Drawing a square*

Objective: Without a stencil, the student will draw 10 squares within the confines of the stimulus area on the paper.

Materials: Same as circle, but with squares of the different lengths of lines.

Prerequisites: Same as for circle.

Child's desired action	*Teacher's action*
1. Picks up pencil.	1. Says, "Pick up the pencil."
2. Positions the pencil point into the right top corner of square.	2. Says, "Put the pencil on the square, here."
3. Moves hand toward left to make top horizontal of the square.	3. Says, "Draw a square."
4. Moves hand downward to make left vertical of the square.	
5. Moves hand from left to right to make bottom horizontal of the square.	
6. Moves hand upward to make right vertical of the square connecting the starting line.	

E. *Drawing a V*

Objective: Without a stencil, the student will draw 10 Vs within the confines of the stimulus area on the paper.

Materials: Same as for circle, but with Vs of different lengths (8, 5, 3", etc.).

Prerequisites: Same as for circle.

Child's desired action	*Teacher's action*
1. Picks up pencil.	1. Says, "Pick up the pencil."
2. Positions the pencil point into the top of the left side of the V.	2. Says, "Put the pencil on the V, here."
	3. Says, "Draw a V."

Table 7–3.   (Continued)

---

3. Draws downward to ver-
   tex.
4. Draws upward on the
   right side of the V.

When the cirterion is met for the standard V, the stencils are rotated, and
Vs pointing upward (∧), to left (<), and to the right (>) are drawn.

F. *Drawing a triangle*
   Objective: Without a stencil, the student will draw 10 isosceles tri-
   angles (△) within the confines of the stimulus area on the paper.
   Materials: Same as for circle, but with isosceles triangles with sides 8,
   5, 3, 1, and 1/4 inch long.
   Prerequisites: Same as for circle.

Child's desired action	Teacher's action
1. Picks up pencil	1. Says, "Pick up the pencil."
2. Positions pencil point into the top vertex of the tri-angle.	2. Says, "Put the pencil on the triangle, here."
3. Moves hand downward down left slope of triangle.	3. Says, "Draw a triangle."
4. Moves hand to right across base of the triangle.	
5. Moves hand upward up right slope of the triangle.	

Once these basic geometric figures have been mastered, you can start to
teach the student the alphabet.

This program was developed by Linda Abbey under my supervision.

guage, and motor skills. These must be improved before
preacademic skills can be taught.

The presentation of material in small steps which are
logically arranged in an easy-to-hard sequence has played
a large part in the success of Brown, Bellamy, and others
in teaching academics to severely handicapped students. It
is strongly recommended that more attention be given to
the work of Blake and associates in teaching reading to
educable retarded students (1973; 1975; 1976). This research evaluated the effects of a number of learning variables on the reading skills of educable retarded students.

The implications for educational practice drawn from the results of these studies may have merit with the severely handicapped.

REFERENCES

Apfel, J. Some TMR's can read. *Education and Training of the Mentally Retarded*, 1975, *9(4)*, 199–200.

Bellamy, C. T., & Brown, L. A sequential procedure for teaching addition skills to trainable retarded students. *Training School Bulletin*, 1972, *69*, 31–44.

Bellamy, G. T., & Buttars, K. Teaching trainable level retarded students to count money toward personal independence through academic instruction. *Education and Training of the Mentally Retarded*, 1975, *10(1)*, 18–25.

Bellamy, G. T., Greiner, C., & Buttars, K. Arithmetic computation for trainable retarded students: Continuing a sequential instructional program. *Training School Bulletin*, 1974, *70(4)*, 230–240.

Blake, K. Special reading instructional procedures for mentally retarded and learning disabled children. *Journal of Research and Development in Education*, Monograph, 1973.

Blake, K. Special reading instructional procedures for mentally retarded and learning disabled children. *Journal of Research and Development in Education*, Monograph, 1975.

Blake, K. Special reading instructional procedures for mentally retarded and learning disabled children. *Journal of Research and Development in Education*, Monograph, 1976.

Brown, L. Instructional programs for trainable level retarded students. In L. Mann & D. Sabatino (Eds.), *The first review of special education*, Vol. 2. Philadelphia: JSE Press, 1973.

Brown, L. & Perlmutter, L. Teaching functional reading to trainable level retarded students. *Education and Training of the Mentally Retarded*, 1971, *6*, 74–84.

Brown, L. & York, R. Developing programs for severely handicapped students: Teacher training and classroom instruction. *Focus on Exceptional Children*, 1974, *6(2)*.

Brown, L., Bellamy, G. T., & Gadberry, E. A procedure for the development and measurement of rudimentary quantitative concepts in low functioning trainable students. *Training School Bulletin*, 1971, *68*, 178–185.

Brown, L., Williams, W., & Crowner, T. *A collection of papers and programs related to public school services for severely handicapped students.* Madison, Wisconsin: Madison Public Schools, 1974, Volume 4.

Brown, L., Crowner, T., Williams, W., & York, R. *Madison's alternative to zero exclusion: A book of readings.* Madison, Wisconsin: Madison Public Schools, 1975, Volume 5.

Brown, L., Scheuerman, N., Cartwright, S., & York, R. *The design and implementation of an empirically based instructional program for severely handicapped students: Toward the rejection of the exclusion principle.* Madison, Wisconsin: Madison Public Schools, 1973, Volume 3.

Brown, L., Hupper, B., Pierce, L., York, R., & Sontag, E. Teaching trainable level retarded students to read unconjugated action verbs. *Journal of Special Education,* 1974, *8(1),* 51–56.

Burton, T. Education for trainables: An impossible dream. *Mental Retardation.* 1974, *12(1),* 45–47.

Corey, J., & Shamow, T. The effects of fading on acquisition and retention of oral reading. *Journal of Applied Behavior Analysis,* 1972, *5,* 311–315.

Coleman, R. A pilot demonstration of the utility of reinforcement techniques in trainable programs. *Education and Training of the Mentally Retarded,* 1970, *5,* 68–70.

Domnie, M., & Brown, L. Teaching severely handicapped students basic reading comprehension skills requiring printed answers to who, what, and where questions. In L. Brown, W. Williams, & T. Crowner (Eds.), *A collection of papers and programs related to public school services for severely handicapped students.* Madison, Wisconsin: Madison Public Schools, 1974.

Dorry, G., & Zeaman, D. The use of a fading technique in paired-associate teaching of a reading vocabulary with retardates. *Mental Retardation,* 1973, *11(6),* 3–6.

Ferritor, D., Buckholdt, D., Hamblin, R., & Smith, L. The noneffects of contingent reinforcement for attending behavior on work accomplished. *Journal of Applied Behavior Analysis,* 1972, *5(1),* 7–18.

Goldberg, I., & Rooke, M. Research and educational practices with mentally deficient children. In N. Haring & R. Schiefelbusch (Eds.), *Methods in special education.* New York: McGraw-Hill, 1967.

Johnson, F., & Brown, L. The use of "whole word" procedures to develop basic components of selected chart story reading skills in severely handicapped young students. In L. Brown, W. Williams, & T. Crowner (Eds.), *A collection of papers and programs related to public school services for severely handicapped students.* Madison, Wisconsin: Madison Public Schools, 1974.

Kirby, F., & Shields, F. Modification of arithmetic response rate and attending behavior in a seventh-grade student. *Journal of Applied Behavior Analysis,* 1972, *5(1),* 79–84.

Lahey, B., McNees, M., & Brown, C. Modification of deficits in reading for comprehension. *Journal of Applied Behavior Analysis,* 1969, *2(1),* 49–53.

Lovitt, T., & Curtiss, K. Effects of manipulating an antecedent event on mathematics response rate. *Journal of Applied Behavior Analysis,* 1968, *1(4),* 329–333.

Lovitt, T., & Curtiss, K. Academic response rate as a function of teacher and self-imposed contingencies. *Journal of Applied Behavior Analysis,* 1969, *2(1),* 49–53.

MacAulay, B. D. A program for teaching speech and beginning reading to nonverbal retardates. In H. N. Sloane & B. D. MacAulay (Eds.), *Operant procedures in remedial speech and language training.* Boston: Houghton Mifflin, 1968.

Resnick, L., Wang, M., & Kaplan, J. Task analysis in curriculum design: A hierarchically sequenced introductory mathematics curriculum. *Journal of Applied Behavior Analysis,* 1973, *6(4),* 679–710.

Sidman, M., & Cresson, O. Reading and cross model transfer of stimulus equivalence in severe retardation. *American Journal of Mental Deficiency,* 1973, *77(5),* 515–523.

Sidman, M., & Stoddard, L. T. The effectiveness of fading in programming a simultaneous form discrimination for retarded children. *Journal of the Experimental Analysis of Behavior,* 1967, *10.*

Sloan, W., & Birch, J. A rationale for degrees of retardation. *American Journal of Mental Deficiency,* 1955, *60,* 258–259.

Staats, A., & Butterfield, W. H. Treatment of reading in a culturally deprived juvenile delinquent: An application of learning principles. *Child Development,* 1965, *4,* 925–942.

Staats, A., Minke, K., Goodwin, R., & Landeen, J. Cognitive behavior modification: Motivated learning reading treatment with subprofessional therapy technicians. *Behavior Research and Therapy,* 1967, *5,* 283–299.

Wehman, P. Direct training of reading skills. *Academic Therapy,* 1977, *12(4),* 463–470.

Williams, W., Coyne, P., Johnson, F., Scheuerman, N., Stepner, J., & Swetlik, F. A rudimentary developmental math skill sequence for severely handicapped students. In L. Brown, W. Williams & T. Crowner (Eds.), *A collection of papers and programs related to public school services for severely handicapped students.* Madison, Wisconsin: Madison Public Schools, 1974.

Chapter 8

RESEARCH AND TRAINING DIRECTIONS WITH THE SEVERELY AND PROFOUNDLY HANDICAPPED

With more and more severely and profoundly handicapped students receiving public school educational services, educators are faced with the problem of deciding what skills to teach, how to teach and maintain skills, and how to measure results (Brown, 1973). The results of research in this area must be translated into educational practice in the classroom (Aserlind, 1969; Blake, 1974; Meyen & Altman, 1976).

Unfortunately, there is little research that addresses these issues and other salient topics such as efficiency of training techniques, comparative research between normals and the retarded, and longitudinal data collection. Training of the severely and profoundly handicapped has typically been reported in clinical program reports or descriptions rather than as research in which a priori hypotheses were formulated and then systematically examined. Although numerous reports describe successful training of the severely and profoundly handicapped (Luckey & Addison, 1974), most of these articles have not identified the issues with which researchers can help teachers or practitioners. This chapter describes several areas of applied research that are critical to the development of educational programming for the severely handicapped as a credible force in the public schools.

RESEARCH AREA 1: NEED FOR LONGITUDINAL DATA

When planning programs for severely and profoundly handicapped students, a *criterion of ultimate functioning* must be identified (Brown, Nietupski, & Hamre-Nietupski, 1977). This criterion is an interdisciplinary assessment and evaluation of the child's long-term potential. If teachers are able to approximate what the least restrictive environment may ultimately be for the student, such as a group home, this will facilitate individual program planning and objectives.

To empirically verify such attempts at long-range planning, it is necessary to have longitudinal data or tracking of students' educational progress from 3 through 21 years of age. In this way the efficacy of programs can be validated and educational personnel will eventually be able to predict a child's potential with more confidence. More importantly, the credibility of training with this population will be either substantiated or found lacking.

Ultimately, the economics of training the severely handicapped must be addressed because the movement toward litigation may begin to boomerang, particularly if parents of nonretarded children begin to protest. With the increased size of regular classes in many cities such a backlash is not altogether improbable.

The question of whether, or how much, severely handicapped persons can contribute to society will also be answered by longitudinal data. In recent work of Levy and associates (1976) in training severely retarded children to perform manual tasks is one example of long-range vocational planning. Since generalized vocational behaviors (that is, acquisition and competitive production across tasks) are rarely acquired by the severely handicapped in a short time, the initial exposure to work training at a relatively young age is a unique programming area which that be examined by teachers.

Many school systems have research and evaluation departments, and usually these departments' work is largely psychometric. It may be advisable for school administrators to utilize research departments to assess and evaluate the behavioral progress of all severely and profoundly handicapped students. With the advent of computer technology, yearly data can be rapidly analyzed and used for administrative decisions as well as funding allotments and program modifications.

RESEARCH AREA 2: INSTRUCTIONAL TECHNOLOGY

This is an area which most of the program reports discussed in previous chapters in this book focused upon. Usually, instructions, modeling, and physical assistance have been used as a means of teacher assistance, and large amounts of social or edible reinforcement are provided as incentives for the development of motor skills (Auxter, 1971), self-care behaviors (Bensberg, Colwell, & Cassell, 1965), language (Snyder, Lovitt, & Smith, 1975), and social skills (Morris & Dolker, 1974). These are typical curriculum content areas for the severely and profoundly handicapped.

While these articles do demonstrate the learning capacities of the severely handicapped, the instructional procedures employed are often not sufficiently clear for others to replicate. Also, the components in this training package have not been isolated to allow individual assessment of their impact. A notable exception to this general rule is a recent study that examined the effects of modeling versus physical guidance on the acquisition of correct utensil use by severely retarded youngsters (Nelson, Cone, & Hanson, 1975). These workers found that modeling alone was insufficient in teaching students how to use utensils correctly.

Only recently have instructional programs for the severely handicapped been presented precisely enough to encourage replication (e.g., Brown, Williams, & Crowner, 1974; Brown, Crowner, Williams, & York, 1975). This work is an excellent model for guiding teachers through training sequences with the severely handicapped because it designates the specific teacher behaviors required for learning.

Those involved in research of optimal instructional technology might also investigate:

- The effects of lives versus symbolic models on the acquisition and maintenance of skills (Wehman, 1976a)
- The role of instructions in developing behavior (Kazdin, Silverman, & Sittler, 1975)
- The manipulation of different parameters of reinforcement and an assessment of changes in adaptive behavior; it cannot be inferred that results of reinforcement programs with less handicapped populations are necessarily generalizable to the severely and profoundly handicapped
- An evaluation of the efficacy of social reinforcement with the profoundly handicapped
- An examination of ways of making reinforcers more attractive and motivating
- An evaluation of whether results of the staff training research with paraprofessionals (e.g., Gardner, 1973) are applicable to classroom teachers.

The efficacy of different materials with the severely and profoundly handicapped must also be examined (Brown &

York, 1974). For example in leisure time programming, some have called for a more systematic selection of play materials (Wehman, 1976b) or for adapting play materials to the child's handicap (Cleland, Swartz, & Chasey, 1971). The choice of academic materials and accompanying activities will play a crucial role in the acquisition and maintenance of different behaviors. Creative researchers may be able to draw on larger populations of severely and profoundly handicapped persons (e.g., institutions) than are typically found in most school systems and may be able to use these individuals as a "test market" for new materials or activities. Consistent with this notion, there should be a move toward commercialized program packages made available to parents or school systems. This is aptly demonstrated by the toothbrushing package promoted by Horner, Billions, and Lent (1975).

Although principles of operant and respondent conditioning are usually involved in the education and training of severely handicapped students, other sources of experimental learning research may influence the acquisition of new skills. For example, specific variables that influence the learning process include contiguity of instances, simultaneous or successive exposure, and relationship of positive to negative instances (Blake, 1974). General learning variables such as amount of material, amount of practice and distribution of practice are other manipulations that may be implemented as well.

What is required are studies that evaluate the effectiveness of the learning variables involved in concept and verbal learning by severely handicapped students. The manipulation of selected antecedent events in concept and verbal learning, in conjunction with careful attention to previously demonstrated applications of operant conditioning, will lead to maximal use of the learning knowledge base in the education process.

RESEARCH AREA 3: ASSESSMENT AND EVALUATION

If there is a commitment to a behavioral model of programming, as it appears there must be for success with the severely handicapped (Gardner, 1971), then data collection and program assessment must be streamlined. Involved time-sampling techniques (Powell, Martindale, & Kulp, 1975), continuous data measures, and precision teaching techniques (Haring & Krug, 1975) may not be convenient or practical for teachers who have limited support services. Recording data periodically is one alternative. Also, researchers might examine which behaviors require continuous data collection.

For example, it would appear that volatile behavior problems should have continuous assessment and monitoring. Alternatively, progress in instructional areas, where gains are made slowly, might be assessed weekly. One critical area which must be investigated is the reliability of teacher recording. Related research supports the concept that the observer's expectancy taints the reliability of observations (Johnston & Bolstad, 1975). Certainly, teachers under pressure to demonstrate progress may be biased in their observations.

Results of instructional programs must be assessed in evaluation designs that allow for the empirical verification of behavior change. Multiple baseline (Kazdin, 1975) and changing criterion designs (Bates, Wehman, & Karan, 1977; Hartmann & Hall, 1976) provide a means of evaluating results, and teachers should be encouraged to use these designs. Innovative researchers might explore the development of designs that are more sophisticated than the typical pre- to post-test evaluation, yet which do not interfere with the learning process as reversal designs do.

RESEARCH AREA 4: EFFICIENCY OF INSTRUCTIONAL TECHNOLOGY

As it becomes evident that the severely handicapped are capable of acquiring new skills once thought beyond their potential, the focus must move to the efficiency of the instructional technology employed. This involves an analysis of the costs for manpower and equipment, the amount of time required for different skills to be learned, and more economical ways of training, such as greater use of parents or the family with preschool children.

A data-based model of programming allows for an analysis of the number of days, weeks, or months involved in acquisition, transfer, and retention of skills. It may be beneficial for researchers to examine data reported for the training of motor, self-help, and language skills with severely and profoundly handicapped subjects in previous studies. Although such data analyses would have to be further categorized by chronological ages of subjects and sample size, approximate trends in training times across skills might be derived. (Such a data analysis of self-help skills is described in Tables 1–1, 1–2, and 1–3.) If researchers can identify such trends, normative data could eventually be established to ensure greater accuracy in predicting student progress and potential.

Similarly, it would be invaluable to assess the amount of manpower required to train students of different ages and behavioral levels. Teacher-student ratios of one-to-five have not been empirically determined, and may not be required if heterogeneous student groupings were decided upon, increased group instruction was found to be practical, or certain skills were identified which did not require extensive individualized instruction. The implications of such findings should be apparent for educational administrators.

Research Area 5: Generalization and Maintenance Training

An oft cited criticism of behavior modification training programs is the situation-specific learning effects of program results and the limited durability of results once contingencies are withdrawn. In recent years, however, transfer of training has been empirically demonstrated in many behavioral training programs (Kazdin, 1975). A recent review of these studies (Wehman, Abramson, & Norman, 1977) revealed that varying stimulus conditions, parent training, use of peers, implementation of naturalistic reinforcers, and fading contingencies are each effective means of promoting generalization and maintenance. These procedures have not been extensively applied in programs with the severely and profoundly handicapped.

Researchers must address themselves to two central questions in this area: (1) Which of the techniques above are most effective and efficient with the severely handicapped, and similarly, what are the limitations of these procedures? Once again, longitudinal, or perhaps cross-sectional data would be invaluable in assessing the efficacy of different strategies to transfer training. (2) What is the potential for self-management training with the severely and profoundly handicapped? In the earlier report (Wehman et al., 1978) self-control studies with the mentally handicapped were not available. Although there have been previous discussions on behavioral self-control with the retarded (Mahoney & Mahoney, 1976; Wehman, 1975), specific training procedures for developing self-regulation in the severely handicapped are as yet unclear. If the severely and profoundly handicapped can acquire self-control, this will greatly alleviate transfer of training problems, decrease the logistical constraints of continual one-to-one instruction, and facilitate independent, self-sufficient behavior.

RESEARCH AREA 6: COMPARATIVE STUDIES

Stainback, Stainback, and Maurer (1976) have observed that, as a basis of curriculum development for the severely and profoundly handicapped, developmental norms of nonretarded infants and children must be closely examined. This is a most fertile area for those interested in basic research with the severely handicapped. It also suggests an increased need for investigators in mental retardation to develop a closer understanding of experimental child psychology and child development.

Many of the research results with nonretarded infants and toddlers may be highly applicable to the development and growth of the severely and profoundly handicapped. Language, cognition, play, and motor development are skill areas which can be comparatively examined. It would be helpful to know whether methods of accelerating development used with "at risk" infants or normal children are similarly effective with the severely handicapped. Early results by Hayden and Haring (1974) give some credence to this notion with mongoloid children who received language stimulation beginning at 3 months of age. These children have subsequently made substantial improvements in language in the past 5 years.

If it is discovered that the severely and profoundly handicapped do develop a sequence similar to that of normal children, as some have already suggested (Woodward, 1959), then a more precise taxonomy of mental retardation may be possible. Hopefully, such research would allow educators to identify behavioral and cognitive characteristics in the severely handicapped which would facilitate prescriptions for learning. In the present classification system, there is far too much heterogeneity of adaptive behavior to allow for sound programming.

Comparative research studies would also provide information on the relative efficacy of different materials and environmental arrangements with the severely handicapped and nonretarded preschoolers. This could give direction to future development of materials and could support the use of open classrooms versus highly structured cubicle learning (Haubrich & Shores, 1976).

SUMMARY

In the concluding section of this chapter, it seems appropriate to outline the research needs which the leading workers in the education of severely handicapped students have identified as critical to classroom programming and planning. A recent paper by Williams and associates (1974) described nine types of information necessary to further our knowledge about programming for the severely and profoundly handicapped:

1. We need information on the longitudinal effects of various program alternatives. For example, it may be the case that students will acquire discriminations more rapidly through an errorless learning paradigm but perhaps the behavior will not readily maintain nor generalize.
2. We need information on how to fit various programming alternatives or branches to specific children.
3. We need information on what to teach these students and in what sequence. For example, perhaps we are getting too much stress too early or out of sequence on object recognition programs.
4. The programs described here were implemented utilizing a low student to teacher ratio (i.e., 1:1–3:1). We need to either develop methods for programming in larger groups or to develop a technology (teaching machines) which can accommodate a low ratio.
5. We need techniques for solving severe management problems in public schools. In institutions shock, food deprivation, restraint, and isolation have been used to establish behavior control. In public school settings there are restrictions on the use of such procedures.

6. If the skills we teach these children are to maintain and generalize, we will need to work closely with parents. We need information on how to facilitate effective parent-school interactions.

7. A key skill to facilitating the independent functioning of these students is expressive language. Thus far we have not been very successful at teaching these students to use functional expressive language.

8. Many of these students are on drugs for medical reasons. We need ways of minimizing drug effects which are detrimental to student performance.

9. We need help in making programs for these students usable by untrained public school teachers. . . . To make programs viable for untrained public school teachers we could:

   a. intensively train teachers in the use of operant analysis and behavior modification procedures.

   b. detect and program for these students at a very young age such that intensive intervention in public schools may be unnecessary.

   c. operationally define and articulate instructional procedures, program content, and sequence to the point where a relatively untrained teacher can read a program and effectively implement it.

(Williams et al., 1974, pp. 36–37)

In short, a great deal of work is ahead before public school programming for the severely and profoundly handicapped advances to the more precise technology that this population requires. Only through increased research and programming will the answers to many of these questions be answered.

REFERENCES

Aserlind, L. Research: Some implications for the classroom. *Teaching Exceptional Children,* 1969, *1,* 42–54.

Auxter, D. Motor skill development in the profoundly retarded. *Training School Bulletin,* 1971, *68,* 5–9.

Bates, P., Wehman, P., & Karan, O. Evaluation of work performance of a developmentally disabled adolescent: Use of a changing criterion design. In O. C. Karan, P. Wehman, A. Renzaglia, & R. Schutz (Eds.), *Habilitation practices with the severely developmentally disabled.* University of Wisconsin Rehabilitation Research and Training Center: Madison, Wisconsin, 1977.

Bensberg, G., Colwell, C., & Cassell, R. Teaching the profoundly retarded self-help activities by behavior shaping techniques. *American Journal of Mental Deficiency,* 1965, *69,* 674–679.

Blake, K. A. *Teaching the retarded.* Englewood Cliffs, NJ: Prentice Hall, 1974.

Brown, L. Instructional programs for the trainable-level retarded students. In L. Mann & D. Sabatino (Eds.), *The first review of special education,* Vol. 2. Philadelphia: JSE Press, 1973.

Brown, L., & York, R. Developing programs for severely handicapped students: Teacher training and classroom instruction. *Focus on Exceptional Children,* 1974, *6(2).*

Brown, L., Nietupski, J. & Hamre-Nietupski, S. The criterion of ultimate functioning and public school services for severely handicapped students. In *Hey don't forget about me: Education's investment in the severely profoundly and multiply handicapped.* Reston, Virginia: Council on Exceptional Children, 1977.

Brown, L., Williams, W. W., & Crowner, T. *A collection of papers and programs related to public school services for severely handicapped students,* Vol. IV. Madison, Wisconsin: Madison Public Schools, 1974.

Brown, L., Crowner, T., Williams, W. W., & York, R. *Madison's alternative to zero exclusion.* Vol. V. Madison, Wisconsin: Madison Public Schools, 1975.

Cleland, C., Swartz, J., & Chasey, W. The role of play games and toys in recreation programming for the moderately and profoundly retarded. *Therapeutic Recreation Journal,* Fourth Quarter, 1971, 152–157.

Gardner, J. M. Training the trainers: A review of research on teaching behavior modification. In R. Rubin, J. Brady, & J. Henderson (Eds.), *Advances in behavior therapy.* New York: Academic Press, 1973.

Gardner, W. I. *Behavior modification in mental retardation.* Chicago: Aldine-Atherton, 1971.

Haring, N., & Krug, D. Evaluation of a program of systematic instructional procedures for extremely poor retarded children. *American Journal of Mental Deficiency,* 1975, *79,* 627–631.

Hartmann, D., & Hall, R. V. The changing criterion design. *Journal of Applied Behavior Analysis,* 1976, *9(4),* 527–532.

Haubrich, P., & Shores, R. Attending behavior and academic performance of emotionally disturbed children. *Exceptional Children,* 1976, *42,* 337–339.

Hayden, A., & Haring, N. Early intervention for high risk infants and young children. Programs for Down syndrome children at the University of Wisconsin. In T. Jjossem (Ed.), *Intervention strategies for risk infants and young children.* Baltimore, Maryland: University Park Press, 1974.

Horner, R. D., Billions, C., & Lent, J. R. *Toothbrushing.* Seattle: Edmark Associates, 1975.

Johnson, S., & Bolstad, O. Reactivity to home observation: A comparison of audio recorded behavior with observers present or absent. *Journal of Applied Behavior Analysis,* 1975, *8,* 181–186.

Kazdin, A. E. *Behavior modification in applied settings.* Homewood, Illinois: Dorsey Press, 1975.

Kazdin, A. E., Silverman, N., & Sittler, J. The use of prompts to enhance vicarious effects of nonverbal approval. *Journal of Applied Behavior Analysis,* 1975, *8,* 279–286.

Levy, S., Pomerantz, D., & Gold, M. W. Work skill development. In N. Haring & L. Brown (Eds.), *Teaching the severely handicapped.* New York: Grune & Stratton, 1976.

Luckey, R., & Addison, M. The profoundly retarded: A new challenge for public education. *Education and Training of the Mentally Retarded,* 1974, *9,* 123–130.

Mahoney, M., & Mahoney, K. Self-control techniques with the mentally retarded. *Exceptional Children,* 1976, *42,* 338–339.

Meyen, E., & Altman, R. Public school programming for the severely/profoundly handicapped: Some researchable problems. *Education and Training of the Mentally Retarded,* 1976, *11(1),* 40–45.

Morris, R., & Dolker, M. Developing cooperative play in socially withdrawn retarded children. *Mental Retardation,* 1974, *12,* 24–27.

Nelson, G., Cone, J., & Hanson, C. Training correct utensil use in retarded children: Modeling vs. physical guidance. *American Journal of Mental Deficiency,* 1975, *80,* 114–122.

Powell, M., Martindale, A., & Kulp, S. An evaluation of time-sample measures of behavior. *Journal of Applied Behavior Analysis,* 1975, *8,* 463–470.

Snyder, L., Lovitt, T., & Smith, J. Language training for the severely retarded: Five years of behavior analysis research. *Exceptional Children,* 1975, *42,* 7–16.

Stainback, S., Stainback, W., & Maurer, S. Training teachers for the severely and profoundly handicapped. A new frontier. *Exceptional Children*, 1976, *42*, 203–210.

Wehman, P. Behavioral self control with the mentally retarded. *Journal of Applied Rehabilitation Counseling*, 1975, *6*, 27–34.

Wehman, P. Imitation as a facilitator of treatment for the mentally handicapped. *Rehabilitation Literature*, 1976, *37*, 41–48 (a).

Wehman, P. Selection of play materials for the severely handicapped: A continuing dilemma. *Education and Training of the Mentally Retarded*, 1976, *11(1)*, 46–51 (b).

Wehman, P., Abramson, M., & Norman, C. Transfer of training in behavior modification programs: An evaluative review. *Journal of Special Education*, 1977, *11(2)*, 217–231.

Wehman, P., Schutz, R., Bates, P., Renzaglia, A., & Karan, O. Self-management programs with mentally retarded workers: implications for developing independent vocational behavior. *British Journal of Social and Clinical Psychology*, 1978, *17(1)*, 58–68.

Williams, W. W., Stepner, J., Scheverman, N., Broome, R., Conte, S., Crowner, T., & Brown, L. A partial delineation of what the practitioner needs from the researcher in developing public school programs for selected low functioning individuals. In L. Brown, W. Williams, & T. Crowner (Eds.), *A collection of papers and programs related to public school services for severely handicapped students*. Madison, Wisconsin: Madison Public Schools, 1974.

Woodward, M. The behavior of idiots interpreted by Piaget's theory of sensorimotor development. *British Journal of Educational Psychology*, 1959, *29*, 60–61.

INDEX